Signs of Spirits

When Loved Ones Visit

By

Joni Mayhan

Cover design by Joni Mayhan

Signs of Spirits Copyright 2016 by Joni Mayhan. All rights reserved. No part of this book may be used or reproduced in any manner without written permission from the author.

Any resemblances to actual places, people (living or dead), or incidents that happened that are not listed are purely coincidental. Prior approval has been obtained from all parties who are mentioned in this book.

Also by Joni Mayhan:

True Paranormal Non-fiction

Spirit Nudges – Allowing Help from the Other Side

Ghost Magnet

Signs of Spirits – When Loved Ones Visit

Ruin of Souls

Ghost Voices (Paranormal 101 Series – Book 1)

Dark and Scary Things – A Sensitive's Guide to the Paranormal World

Bones in the Basement – Surviving the S.K. Haunted Victorian Mansion

The Soul Collector

Devil's Toy Box

Ghostly Defenses – A Sensitive's Guide for Protection

Paranormal Fiction

Lightning Strikes (Angels of Ember Dystopian Trilogy– Book 1)

Ember Rain (Angels of Ember Dystopian Trilogy – Book 2)

Angel Storm (Angels of Ember Dystopian Trilogy – Book 3)

The Spirit Board (Winter Woods – Book 1)

The Labyrinth (Winter Woods – Book 2)

The Corvus (Winter Woods – Book 3)

Acknowledgements

The concept for this book began with an article I wrote for The Ghost Diaries (theghostdiaries.com). I've been writing for them for nearly a year and am always pleased when an article hits its mark. When the Dead Come Calling – Signs That a Deceased Loved One is Nearby did far more than hitting a mark. It went viral. It was shared over a million times by people all over the world.

Soon after that, people began contacting me with their personal stories. I received so many stories; I knew I had to do something with them. I couldn't just read them and move on with my life. It felt essential that I shared them with others.

My first thank you goes to Jared Salas and Jake Anderson of The Ghost Diaries for giving me a platform to share my articles. My second thank you goes to all the wonderful people who shared stories with me. I was blown away by them.

I would also like to thank my dedicated beta readers: Gare Allen, Raymond Richard, Rosa McRae Yellig and Ken Murray. Your input was incredibly valuable.

Since this is my fifteenth published book, I want to also thank my friends, family and fans for always supporting me, and for expanding your bookshelves to accommodate my growing collection. Being a writer can be a lonely job, but it wasn't the case for this book. I was surrounded by people who were eager to help.

Lastly, I want to thank Barbara Williams. She started out being my mentor and ended up being my friend. It's so wonderful to be blessed with access to her wisdom and knowledge. You are amazing, Barbara, and I will shout it to the world.

Contents

Chapter 1 - My Story

*W*hen I was six years-old, my life was perfect. I lived with my family in a small rustic cabin that was nestled beside a picturesque pond.

Behind the cabin was a hundred acres of untouched woodlands, filled to the brim with singing birds and wild rabbits that often nibbled the clover at the edge of our yard. I had a swing set in the backyard, where I learned to mimic the Bobwhite Quail, and a big collie dog named Sam who followed me everywhere I went. Best of all though, I had easy access to my adoring grandparents.

Nanny and Poppy lived in a house across the pond from us, separated by a long narrow dam that served as a gateway to all that was good and safe in the world. Crossing the dam was like moving into another world, one where I was the princess of the castle.

Nanny would drop everything to sit on the floor and play with me, while Poppy often took me for long walks through the woods, sharing his love of nature.

There were a myriad of paths in the woods behind our house. I can remember tipping my head up to look at the sunshine that parted through the high branches of the trees as the blue jays scolded us for disturbing their sanctuary.

As we walked, Poppy told me stories about Big Lake, which was hidden in the center of the woods and how people would flock to the lake to swim during the humid Indiana summers. He showed me a massive old oak tree that was carved with faded initials of people who probably weren't even still alive. When I asked him to carve my initials into the tree, he refused.

"You don't want to be one of the crowd. Let's start your own tree," he told me and carved my initials on another tree.

When I was with them, I felt cherished and safe. The feeling was warm and intoxicating, something I've never felt since. I never dreamed that it would all go away so quickly.

Even as a small child, I knew that Nanny had a bad heart. She had scarlet fever when she was younger, something that damaged her heart beyond repair. One night, she went to bed and simply never woke up again. Nanny died at the age of 53, just one year older than I am right now.

While her death wasn't unexpected, it still left a gaping hole in all our lives. It probably hit me the hardest. No longer could I race across the dam to spend the day playing with her. Walking into her house felt empty and sad.

Several nights after her death, I had a dream that I will never forget. In the dream, my mother and I went to her house to clean out her closet. My mother wanted to donate her clothing to a charity and sort through her belongings to collect a few remembrances.

The details in my dream were so crisp, it was difficult to comprehend that it wasn't actually happening. As we came through the door, I could feel the warmth of the heat on my face and could smell the familiar scent of her house. Nanny's small dog Skipper greeted us with sniffs and tail wagging, smelling vaguely of flea powder as her nails clicked on the tile floor. I looked up at my mother beside me. She was distracted and short tempered. Her dark hair was held back beneath an old yellow handkerchief that was tied at the nape of her neck and her face was puffy and red from crying.

As we came through the doorway, I was astounded to find Nanny sitting on the couch. My mother walked right past her and headed to her bedroom, something I found incomprehensible.

Was it possible that my mother couldn't see Nanny?

I raced to the couch and wrapped my arms around my grandmother's neck.

"Nanny! Nanny! I thought you were dead!" I cried, tears rushing down my cheeks.

She pulled me away and looked lovingly into my eyes and said something that will remain with me for the rest of my life.

"I did die, Joni," she said. "But I couldn't leave without saying goodbye to you." She told me she loved me and then I woke up from the dream, my pillow wet with tears.

I've come to understand that loved ones often remain with us throughout our lives, offering comfort and reassurance when we need it the most, but I wouldn't understand this until I was much older.

The next time I felt Nanny was when I was eighteen years-old.

I was a rebellious teenager, so it came as no surprise to anyone that I decided to buck the system and take a year off of school after graduating from high school. Many of my friends were going away to college, but I was restless to get

3

my life started. I was bored with school and wanted a break before diving into college.

I moved out of my parent's home the day after I graduated from high school and was eager to get going on my future. I had my eye on an apartment across town and needed a job to pay the bills.

The first interview on my list went well. It wasn't a job I saw myself doing for the rest of my life, but it would bring in enough money to give me the freedom I so desperately yearned for.

As I was racing home, I pushed past the speed limit, loving the way the wind poured through the windows. My beloved car was a machine made for speed. When I stepped on the accelerator, it responded like a race horse released from the chute. Without warning, Nanny's face appeared in my mind and screamed, "Slow down!" in my mind.

The encounter was so startling, I found myself responding to her words. I slammed my foot on the brake and brought my speed down. As soon as I reached the lower speed, my front tire blew out.

I coasted to the side of the road, my mind numb.

I might have only been eighteen years-old, but I knew enough about cars to know how powerful that moment was. If my tire had blown out while I was driving 70 miles per hour, I probably would have flipped the car and might not have survived the accident.

"Thank you, Nanny," I whispered, feeling my heart pound heavily in my chest.

Since that time, I've felt Nanny with me more frequently. Sometimes I hear her voice, mixed in with my own internal dialogue.

4

If I'm sitting in front of my computer when I should be getting ready to leave for class, her voice is the one that prompts me to get in the shower. If I'm driving too fast, she tells me to slow down.

It took me years to understand that what I was hearing wasn't my own chatter. Nanny has been with me in more ways than one.

Just days ago, I found myself in a panic as I drove with an empty gas tank, looking for a gas station.

"You will make it. It's going to be okay." I heard the voice in my head as clearly as though it were whispered in my ear. Moments later, I coasted into the gas station, mere miles away from running out of gas.

Most people base their expectations by what they see on television and in the movies. In those heightened examples, the loved one appears fully formed and stands in front of the grieving relative to pass along a message or offer comfort. Real life is seldom so clear.

A sign could be as subtle as a certain song coming on the radio when you're thinking about that person. It could be a bright red cardinal landing on a tree branch outside your window. It could even be an unexpected phone call from a friend, asking you to join her for coffee. Sometimes the signs are even more elusive.

I believe that Nanny jumped in my mind to warn me about my impending tire blow-out in a way that would capture my full attention, but she's given me other signs that are much harder to attribute to her.

There was a time when I was dating and was torn between two men. As I drove to work one day thinking about it, I heard a voice in my head that said, "Neither one of those men will be in your life."

It startled me on two accounts. Firstly, I'm a hopeless romantic who can't get out of her own way. It would never occur to me that I wouldn't end up with one of those men. Secondly, was the word usage. Neither one of those men will be in YOUR life. Surely, if the thought was coming from my own internal dialogue I would have thought MY instead of YOUR, right?

Nanny has come to me other times as well, offering comforting words and nudging me when I needed to be nudged. I didn't realize it was her voice because I was only six years old when she died. I didn't know her well enough to recognize her personality.

Once I suspected it was Nanny, I asked my mother about my grandmother. "Was Nanny the kind of person who would lovingly nag you to do something you were supposed to do?" I asked her. In many ways, I probably didn't need to even ask. My mother, who was Nanny's daughter, often said the same things to me when I was younger.

"Joni! You need to leave or you're going to be late for school!" was something I heard hundreds, if not thousands of times. She probably learned that behavior from her own mother.

My mother was quick to confirm it. Yes. Nanny was motherly and was an adept parent. It probably drove her crazy that I was sitting at my computer, mindlessly scrolling through Facebook when there were dirty dishes in the sink, an unmade bed and fifteen minutes left before I needed to leave the house. In her day, life was different. There weren't as many mindless distractions, and people tended to be more diligent about their responsibilities. Watching me goof off probably didn't sit well with her.

While I was close with Poppy too, I don't feel him near me as often. I can only recall one instance where I feel he was with me and it's something I've often reduced down to circumstance.

I was seventeen years old and was driving home from my boyfriend's house. Several of his friends knew of a road that was thought to be haunted, so we checked it out. While we were there, we saw a strange mist appear at the end of the road, something that freaked us out more than a little. My boyfriend and I couldn't get in our cars fast enough. My car was parked at his parent's house, so I left soon after we got there. With the thought of ghosts in my mind, I drove home, still feeling the chill from our experience.

The drive from his house to mine took me down a long dark highway. As I drove, I kept looking towards the side of the road for the same sort of mist I saw on the haunted road. Several times, I even thought I saw something in my backseat. I turned the dome light on and whipped around in my seat, nearly sending myself sailing off the road. After the third time of this, I saw a pair of headlights in my rear view mirror.

I narrowed my eyes at them, not remembering seeing a car behind me before that. I'd been on the highway for nearly fifteen minutes without seeing another car. Instead of feeling anxious, worried that someone was following me, I felt a sense of comfort instead. It almost felt as though someone was escorting me home.

As I drove, I played around with my speed to see if the person was really following me or not. I would speed up and the car behind me would speed up. When I slowed down, so did the car. After a while, I just finally settled in for the drive. As soon as I reached the town limits and the bright lights greeted me, the car turned down a side street. I nearly gasped as I watched it in my rear view mirror. It was a caramel colored El Camino, the same exact car Poppy used to drive.

I'll never know for sure if it was Poppy or not, but it doesn't matter. All that matters is the fact that it made me feel safe and removed a lot of the anxiety I was feeling. If it wasn't a phantom car, maybe Poppy had encouraged the person driving the El Camino to follow behind me. It's hard to say. Either way, I'd like to remember it as a sign of his love for me.

A lot of what I experienced in these instances is what led me to begin studying the paranormal. I knew there was more to death than a funeral and some wonderful memories. Proof came to me more times than I could discount.

Sometimes, you have to throw skepticism out the window and listen to your heart instead.

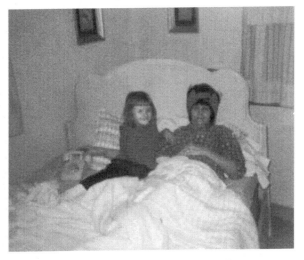

(Above) Joni with Nanny in her bedroom

Chapter 2 - What Death Looks Like

*D*eath is often a taboo subject, even though it's a normal part of our human existence. No one can escape it. Some find it earlier than others, but we all are forced to experience it at one point or another.

If you believe that life ends at death, I feel sorry for you. From my years of studying the paranormal world and talking with psychic mediums, as well as my own spirit guides, I have a far different philosophy.

In many ways, death is really a beginning. It's the ending of one life, but marks our return back to the Astral Plane, a place some people call Heaven. It's where we go to rest from the experiences of our physical lives and to learn and advance our spirits.

I remember the first time I heard about the concept of reincarnation. I was astounded at the thought, but it made tremendous sense to me. Since that point, I've heard dozens of stories about people who have remembered some of their past lives. Through several past life regressions, where I enter a light meditative state, I have uncovered several of mine as well. They were remarkable experiences and helped me understand more about my own soul's journey.

The soul is eternal and never dies. It merely moves from one incarnation to another. There is an afterlife that we go to when we die and it has very little in common with what we learned on a pew.

The White Light

When we die, we often see a beautiful white light before us. It is the most wondrous thing we've ever seen and we find ourselves gravitating towards it without fear.

The light beckons us, filling us with a sense of peace. As we walk towards it, we often forget all about our human lives. We are intoxicated by the sensation and nothing else matters. If we felt pain at the end of our lives, it is quickly forgotten. Everything falls away. Loved ones who have passed away before us often shepherd us into it, guiding us with a gentle touch.

Once we get to the other side, we find ourselves in a place that is filled with love and light. Some people call this place Heaven. People often see it differently, depending on their situation. If you endured a traumatic death, you might find yourself in a hospital where you can heal. Others find themselves in a place unlike any Heaven they've ever imagined. There are houses and people. You can take classes or just mingle with loved ones you haven't seen for a while. You might also be reunited with pets you've lost over the years.

There isn't a saint stationed at the Pearly Gates, deciding whether your elevator goes up or down. There's no judgement, only love. For some of us, this is a tremendous relief. I was raised with the belief that if you were good, you went to Heaven. If you were bad, you went to Hell. There was no middle ground, no place for someone who might have been a little bit of both.

If I'm being brutally honest, it's difficult to evaluate good from bad in some cases. Things that were considered bad back in the eighteen hundreds are now considered normal by today's standards. If a woman in 1850 went to the swimming hole dressed in a modern day bikini, she would be labeled as a harlot. Someone who stole food to feed a starving family might be given some slack, as well. We are all humans and we suffer from the human condition. We make choices based on our needs and our preconceived notions of what good and bad look like. In one household it might be okay to scream and use profanity, while in another house it would be considered a sin.

For me, this concept is far more pleasant than the Heaven or Hell option. It resonates with me, making me realize that good and bad are far too subjective to toss us into one category or another. Good people sometimes do bad things and vice versa. We are humans. We make mistakes and we also rise above our own nature at times. It also makes me happy to believe that our God is a kind and forgiving god, and that perhaps, love and light mean something after all.

All those years in Sunday school taught me to fear my maker, to see him as someone who loved me, but wouldn't flinch at doling out punishment if I didn't follow the rules my church prescribed for me. In time, I've learned that religion is more man-made than God-made, but is essential nonetheless. Imagine the melee if people didn't have the fear of Hell in their heart, even a little bit?

I've learned to become more spiritual than religious. Since I've been studying the paranormal world, I've prayed far more than I ever did before my induction. I've learned that angels guide and protect us and that God loves us no matter what we do.

Our Life Reviews

After you've had a chance to settle in, you meet with your spirit guides to go through a life review. During this time you experience everything you did during your life. It might play in your mind like a movie. You not only see the choices you made, you also see the impact it had on others.

You alone are the judge and jury. If you did something right, you can feel good about it. If you did something wrong, you see the opportunities to improve upon the decision.

A big part of our life review includes an evaluation on our life goals. Whether we realize it or not, we actually choose the life we lived. Before we reincarnated into it, we sat down with our spirit guides, angels and our ancestors and we made a plan. Our overall goal is to become the best soul possible, so we might have set up a scenario that would help us improve upon it.

If we have an issue with patience, we might choose a life filled with long lines, urgent needs and pushy people. If we chose to learn how to better handle power, we might be given a life filled with leadership roles. We won't remember any of this because we are expected to learn from scratch. While it would be much easier to return with the knowledge of our past incarnations, it wouldn't be a fair training lesson.

Once we complete our review, we are encouraged to spend time in this place. We can either socialize with our passed-on loved ones or we can simply learn and grow. We can take classes, enjoy sunsets, play with our pets, grow a garden or begin planning our next incarnation.

We are allowed to stay here for as long as we wish. Many souls might remain in this place for long durations because time really doesn't exist there. The notion of checking our watches fades with death. Time is immeasurable and completely irrelevant.

After we've finished here, we have a choice. We can either stay here to watch over our living loved ones or we can choose to reincarnate into new lives. From what I've learned, most souls decide to stay, at least until their loved ones have passed on. These are the souls who come to visit us, the ones who give us comfort when we need it.

I will admit to the fact that there's so much we don't know. Typically, people don't go through the white light and come back with a full report. In some ways, I believe there are rules they must follow. Some secrets are not theirs to tell. They are here to guide us and comfort us, but they aren't here to provide us with information we aren't meant to know.

Chapter 3 – Ghosts versus Spirits

When we reach out, hoping for communication with a deceased loved one, we have to make sure we know who we're talking to. There is a difference between a spirit and a ghost.

A spirit is someone who has crossed over into the light and has gone to Heaven. They've received divine inspiration and have undergone training. If they reach out to you, they are probably someone you once cared about or someone in your ancestral background. Best of all, you can trust them. They have nothing but your best interest at heart.

A ghost is a soul who refused to cross over into the light and has chosen to remain earth-bound instead. They haven't received any heavenly enlightenment. They are little more than people without bodies. You shouldn't trust them because you don't know for certain who they are. Many ghosts will pretend to be someone else in attempts to gain your trust.

Ask relevant questions that only your loved one knows the answer to. If you get an answer that isn't right, then stop the communication. Ghosts will lie, just like some people will lie. Don't allow yourself to be swayed, even if it's something you truly long for.

As I've discussed in many of my other books, souls often have reasons for not wanting to cross over. In some cases, they feel guilty for something they've done during their lifetimes while others remain because they are fearful that things won't be handled properly.

(Above) Barbara Williams

One of my mentors is a talented psychic medium named Barbara Williams. She feels that sometimes people latch onto something because they simply don't trust anyone else to handle it like they would. "Sometimes they're tied to something because they built it. Whether it was a business, or a house or something they have a very close tie to," she said.

This makes me think about the man who haunted a house I lived in years ago. Once we started renovating the basement, the haunting became unbearable. If he remained earth-bound instead of crossing over because he wanted to look after his house, we certainly angered him when we tore out his work bench in the basement. He wasn't shy about letting us know about it either.

"Many times, they will not cross over because of that. They have to be very gently prompted to cross over. It's very difficult for them to release the hold," Barbara added.

This is an important lesson for people with loved ones who are in the process of dying. In order to move onto the next journey in their lives, they have to learn to let go of this life.

Many people hold on for longer than necessary because they don't understand the process. What happens here in this lifetime is a lesson, something we use to grow and learn. It isn't the only life we'll live. We have to let go in order to move on.

Barbara's own father had a difficult time passing for a similar reason. She sat with him in the hospital, day and night, for a week. He held on tenaciously because he felt that certain people needed him. She wasn't sure what was keeping him alive. Physically, he should have died. He held on until a particular holiday had passed.

As both a psychic medium and a registered nurse, Barbara sees this frequently and tries to bridge the gap when she can. She tries to give people a better understanding of what the dying person is going through and what they might need to hear in order to be able to let go.

She recommends talking with the person, whether you think they can hear you or not (they can, by the way), and tell them that it's going to be okay. "Tell them that you'll be sad, but you'll be okay. There's a great opportunity for them to assist that person in crossing over," she said.

I agree with her wholeheartedly. It's much better to talk to them before they die than to wait until after they've died and remained earth-bound. It's far easier for someone to cross over when they die than it is to attempt it later. Often, the longer they remain on the wrong side of the veil, the more they begin to forget who they were and why they stayed. They're just here.

As a paranormal investigator, I've encountered hundreds of these souls. They might have had their reasons for avoiding the white light, but many of them have been lingering around for decades, if not centuries.

People sometimes attempt to do EVP (Electronic Voice Phenomenon) sessions to communicate with a deceased loved one. This process involves using a standard digital voice recorder. You ask questions and record the dead space between questions, often catching voices of the dead when the audio is played back.

When people try this and get a response, they are often elated, thinking they've made communication with a loved one, but some caution should be employed here. According to Barbara, the response probably didn't come from a passed on loved one. A spirit would feel no need to respond to a question in that capacity.

"They have a whole different purpose and function," she said. "They would reach out to you in other ways," she added. Their communication always has a higher vibration to it. They might come to you in dreams, in images, thoughts or in other ways that we'll delve into in future chapters.

The complexities of the paranormal world are vast and elusive. If someone claims to have absolute knowledge of what really happens, they must have a better connection than most of us do. Realistically, we don't know. We can take information we've collected from various psychic mediums and from our own personal accounts and compile theories, but we won't truly know the truth until we go through it ourselves.

That's why I love the paranormal world so much. It is a mystery to investigate, a puzzle to piece together. It's something we can all work on together and learn as much as we can.

A few days after Andrea's mother passed away, she woke up to hear the sound of a crow singing outside her window. She opened her eyes and just lay there for a moment as she attempted to fully wake up. She started to rise from bed when she realized the room was filled with the scent of lavender, which was her mother's favorite scent.

She smiled, instinctively knowing it was her mother.

Her mother always believed that crows carried the soul of the dead away and often brought them back to loved ones for a visit before crossing over to the other side. It made perfect sense that her mother would send her those two signs.

Many people are dismayed when they don't receive a sign of their loved one shortly after passing. Much of this might be due to the spirit itself.

According to psychic medium Barbara Williams, it depends on the spirit. "I have contacted spirits as soon as a week, but the conversations haven't been lengthy since they do not have much energy for a while. It takes at least a few months to a year for them to build up enough energy for a longer visit."

While the soul is eternal, this doesn't mean the recently deceased are willing, or even capable, of communication, especially if their deaths were difficult or unexpected. It often takes them time to come to terms with what has happened to them. When they're ready, they will reach out to those they wish to communicate with. "They would contact loved ones first, not people they don't know," Barbara added.

If the death was sudden or traumatic, it might take them even longer to return. According to psychic medium Raymond Richard, "They don't immediately go to where everyone else goes. Their souls go to a place where they can heal first." This is especially true for people who took their own lives. They need enough time to mend before they can move on.

If this is the case, the sign might be fleeting in nature. People often miss them because they aren't what they were expecting them to be.

Our logical minds take the information and find a sensible explanation for it, even if it truly doesn't fit. It's easier for us to rationalize it, instead of seeing it for what it really is.

Other people will attempt to rush the process, becoming quickly dismayed when the results don't match their expectations.

If you reach out to them when you're going through an especially difficult time, they might not respond to you. This is because they realize that we are given difficult situations to help us grow. If they interfere or make it easier for us, we will not learn the lesson in order to grow.

"People often have these perceptions that we go through life and everything is supposed to be really wonderful and then we die. Those are really useless lives, because we haven't really done much. There've been no major lessons," Barbara told me.

If it's something they can help you with, they will. If they can't, then it's a lesson you need to learn yourself.

"If you have a higher purpose in life, there are times when you will get divine intervention. It might not even be something you recognize. It might be as simple as you being marked to have a conversation with someone in your future who is going to make a difference in the world. You may never know who that is or what that was," Barbara said.

This is frustrating for many of us, because the people we are asking for help are the same people who would have gladly helped us when they were alive. We have the same expectations of them as we would when they were living. What we don't realize is that they are helping us more by doing nothing. They are forcing us to find the solution ourselves. If they made it easy on us, we would never learn our life lessons, nor would we grow stronger.

I told Barbara the story about how Nanny gave me a warning just before my tire blew out. If our loved ones can't interfere with our life plan, then why did she warn me? Barbara's explanation was truly thought provoking.

According to Barbara, throughout our lives, we have a series of "exit points." These are times when we could naturally leave our bodies and die. We might not always be conscious of the option presented to us, but our soul is aware of them. In my case, even though I wasn't knowingly aware of it, my spirit did not chose to take that exit point, so Nanny was allowed to intervene.

Barbara shared a similar story where she met an exit point, but was allowed to deny it.

She and her husband Steve were driving in their truck going 65 mph when Barbara saw something go past them on the right side of the truck.

Steve saw it too and slowed down. When he got out of the truck and walked around to look at the back of the truck, he discovered that it was their entire back tire. It somehow came off the truck and rolled past them. The truck didn't dip down, nor did they lose control. They were allowed to slow down to a stop.

"When you have a larger life compass or the potential of accomplishing something bigger, your soul knows not to take that exit point," she said.

Starting the line of communication isn't always easy, but you have to have a starting place. If you wish to communicate with a passed on loved one, simply ask them to come to you. If they are capable and it is in your best interest, they will come to you. You just have to recognize the signs.

One thing to look for is signs of old habits coming back into play.

Was your father always complaining about people leaving the lights on in rooms after they left? One way he might let you know he's there is to frequently turn the lights off, sometimes even while you're still in the room. Was your grandmother fussy about where things went? If you rearranged her items, you might find them back in their old familiar locations.

Always bear in mind that it takes a tremendous amount of energy for spirits to manipulate the physical world. If you ask for a sign, look for the subtle signs as well as the obvious. If your best friend always called you on the phone on Thursdays, you might not receive a phantom phone call, but you might notice difficulties with the phone itself.

One of my friends received a phone call from her brother, who had died months previously. As she stared at the screen, reading his name, the call ended before she could pick it up.

When she told me the story, she asked that I didn't use her name because she was fearful that other family members would think she had completely lost her mind.

After the call, she checked with her parents to find out if the phone was still activated, thinking that perhaps someone pressed a button by accident. What she learned left her shaken and confused. The phone number had been deactivated a week after his death.

She went to their house to look at his phone, just to check it out for herself and discovered that the battery was dead. If it was anything like her phone, it probably lost the charge several days after his death. There was no way a call could have been made from his phone.

***

One story that was relayed to me involved window shades. Mary's mother always opened the shades in the house each day to brighten the house with sunshine. After her mother's death, Mary came to check on the house frequently and always found the shades up, despite her attempts to keep them closed. Was her mother coming back to repeat her daily habits?

In a situation like this, most people would look for a logical explanation. It's human nature to make sense of the abnormal because the truth can be daunting and also a bit scary.

We're used to the physical world, where science can explain the events of the day. When something happens that we can't explain, we often close our eyes to it because it scares us.

The signs are all around us, if we know where to look.

Chapter 5 – Strange Synchronicities

Several nights ago as I prepared to go to bed, I couldn't find my cell phone. I'm habitual in my actions, so it seemed strange to me that I couldn't find it. If it's not in my pocket, it is typically plugged into the charger near my nightstand.

I was exhausted, but I couldn't rest without knowing that my phone would be beside me while I slept. I like the safety of having it nearby, along with the ability to know the time, since I've long done away with alarm clocks that tend to taunt me all night with their blaring red numbers.

I started looking in all the normal places. I checked my desk, but didn't find it there. I then looked in the bathroom and my bedroom again. No phone. The only other place it could possibly be was the coffee table that was downstairs in the living room. I heaved a sigh. It wasn't like the living room was fifty miles away, but it did mean that I'd have to walk downstairs to search for it, something I didn't want to do. All I wanted to do was climb into my bed and drift off into a peaceful slumber.

I put on my slippers, waded through my escort of four hungry cats who thought it might be a good time for a midnight snack, and made my way down the stairs to the first floor. As I passed the front door, I noticed it was unlocked.

I am a stickler about locking doors. My son thinks it's silly and would have no problem never locking the door, but my past experiences haunt me and prevent me from trusting my fellow man. When I was fifteen years-old, my mother was pursued by a stalker who often called the house and threatened to kill her and her daughters. The situation became so frightening, the police were involved and tracers were put on our phone and alarms installed in our house. After that experience, living in a house with unlocked doors was as foreign to me as the notion of sleeping on the front lawn. I quickly locked the door and then found my cell phone on the coffee table.

It snowed that night, so the footprints on the front walk were undeniable. When I got up the next morning, I looked out the window and saw them trailing up the walk and stopping at the front door. Had someone attempted to break in, but found the door locked? It wasn't the mailman or a delivery person because no packages were left outside the door. I'll never know for certain, but I do know that someone was looking out for me.

If this happened to most people, they wouldn't even make the connection. They would believe that they accidentally left their cell phones on the table and that the footprints in the snow meant nothing. They would have gone on with their lives, never knowing that someone was protecting them. I knew because I watch for these strange synchronicities. I see them every day.

If I'm attempting to complete some task or obligation and it continues to become exceedingly difficult, I will often stop and evaluate the situation. Many times, this is a sign, given to me by my spiritual allies, which could include passed-on loved ones or spirit guides. They are trying to give me a message. By making things difficult, they could be telling me something. The message could be as simple as "do it another way" or as prevalent as "don't do that." I almost always listen.

Barbara Williams feels that the synchronicities might not always be obvious.

"It might look like chaos from a close perspective, but the further away the perspective, the more it makes sense. There is a linear order to things," she said.

Don't think for a moment that it was coincidence that led you to the so-called chance meeting that changed your life. Think about your life, viewing it through the rear-view mirror. Was there ever a time when you really needed guidance, only to have exactly the right person come along to provide it for you? Mine came right after I wrote my 2014 book *Bones in the Basement - Surviving the SK Pierce Haunted Victorian Mansion.*

A small local metaphysical shop offered to set up a book signing for me and I graciously accepted. While I was there, the shopkeeper noticed that many people were coming in and asking me questions about the paranormal world. We decided to set up a few Paranormal 101 classes, which led to me meeting a group of people who have become like family to me. I really needed those wonderful people to come into my life. While it's easy to say that one thing simply led to another, I believe that one of my loved ones was providing the proper nudges to make sure it happened.

Another example of this also involves my class. Lisa had a few friends, but none who shared her spiritual beliefs. Mere weeks after she started coming to our classes, her husband passed away. The group was wonderfully supportive, going to her house to sit with her and offering her support and friendship at a time when she needed it the most. A psychic medium from our group gave her helpful messages from her husband, helping her understand the depths of his love.

It might be a stretch of the imagination, but I believe that the notion of writing this book was also a sign.

I frequently write for an online paranormal website called The Ghost Diaries (*theghostdiaries.com*). I always try to come up with interesting topics to cover, but none was more popular than the one that talked about connecting with deceased loved ones.

When the Dead Come Calling – Signs That a Deceased Loved One is Nearby went viral. Not only did more than a million people read it, it was shared (and in some cases, blatantly stolen and plagiarized) by many other websites. I was surprised by the popularity it garnered, but was also pleased as well. One of the owners of The Ghost Diaries suggested that I turn it into a book. At the time, I was still in the middle of writing *Ruin of Souls*, but as soon as I finished and took a few weeks off, I found myself thinking about it in earnest.

The more I thought about writing it, the more I couldn't ignore the pull. I began wondering if this too was a sign. Will my works make an impact on someone reading it, changing their life in the process? I guess time will tell.

As I began researching for this book, I went back to my original Ghost Diaries article that kicked it all off and scrolled through the comments.

Some of the people who commented on my story had fascinating stories. I wanted to learn more, so I looked up several of the people on social media and sent them messages. While most of the people didn't respond to my messages, one woman did. I have a funny feeling that as time progresses, I will wonder if she was sent to me or if I was sent to her. Sometimes these things have an interesting way of working out. Here is the message that Paula Braman-Duarte sent me:

"Funny, you should ask for the story and the photo. Wednesday would have been my mom's ninety-seventh birthday and I was going to put a photo of her on Facebook and then thought I'd wait for #TBT (Throw Back Thursday). Then, I kept dithering about it all yesterday morning and then I saw this message from you late in the afternoon.

Mom had been on my mind all week with it being her birthday week and because I always associate the month with her. And it has been so bitter cold which was always the case around her birthday. Further, we are expecting some kind of major snow in New England and we would have a big storm right on or around her birthday without fail! Then, to top it off, after I saw your message I had to go out and while I was driving alone and thinking about giving you a picture, a Bruno Mars song came on the radio.

The lyrics stopped me cold in my thinking as I heard: "girl, you're amazing/ Just the way you are" - I just knew it was a message from my mom because she was always my biggest cheerleader and best friend. How's that for: weird, coincidental, serendipitous, reassuring and amazing? Really, all these things together - I just couldn't get over it!"

What is also interesting to me is the fact that Paula only lives an hour and a half from me. The owners of the Ghost Diaries live on the West Coast and the website is seen by people all over the world. Is it coincidence that the one person who responded to my message lives close to me? I think so.

Here is the story that Paula originally shared with me.

Paula's Story

I have experienced so many of the examples on this list that it is uncanny. One of my favorites being one that happened two days after my mom had passed.

I was busy getting the funeral arrangements finalized so I was out and about early with a long morning of errands. All I could think about was having my (current) favorite sandwich for lunch - very specifically, a turkey with mustard and Swiss cheese on a bulky roll. Very odd that such a thought would be running through my head at that time, and I definitely had none of the ingredients on hand.

I got home, arms full of things, mind on overdrive, only to be met by an old friend and long-ago neighbor. This was someone who had been close to our family, but we had not seen much of in recent years. She had been thinking of me and wanted to drop off lunch. The sandwich she handed me was "as ordered" right down to the bulky roll. I knew immediately it was a sign from my mom that all would be well.

Some people might scoff at some of the stories and say that they're just coincidence. As far as we know, some of it could be random scenarios playing out in a way that causes us to analyze them, but many of them aren't.

Spirits reach out to us in any way they can. It must be quite difficult for them to garner our attention. Imagine trying to wield your way through someone's cluttered thoughts to pass along a message. Often times, the message will be denied because the person receiving it doesn't believe it to be true.

When people come to me with their visitation stories, I always ask them, "What was the first thing you thought about when you received the message?" In the example above, Paula immediately thought about her mother. The thought was linked to the action, which gives it far more relevance. If she didn't connect the dots, then it probably wouldn't have been a message. Her mother made sure that the situation came with the thought of her, almost like putting a name label on a carefully wrapped gift.

Our loved ones often work behind the scenes, pulling all the right strings to make sure we meet the people that we need to meet, when we need to meet them.

I often think about my first "chance meeting" with Barbara Williams. It was an encounter that would completely change the direction of my life.

During the year and a half before I met her, I had been working on a book. It wasn't my first book, by no means. I had written seven books before that one, all of which never made it past my computer screen.

In previous years, it was exceedingly difficult to get a book published. You couldn't even begin the process until you landed a literary agent, something that was harder to manage than getting struck by lightning, something I was painfully aware of.

After sending out hundreds of query letters, one agent asked for sample chapters. Three months after those were sent, she asked for the full manuscript. I mailed it out days later and began counting the months before she finally responded.

She loved it, but wanted me to make a few changes. Enthusiastically, I made those changes and sent it back her within a few weeks. More months went by before I received her response.

She liked the changes, but also wanted me to change something else. This went on for over a year until one day she emailed to tell me that despite the promise the book held, that it wasn't for her. She was going to pass on the project.

I was devastated. Having already been through this same process seven times before with my other books, I wasn't sure I had it in me to try again.

I posted my dismay on social media, feeling the weight of the world on my shoulders. One of my friends suggested that I self-publish the book myself.

I immediately began researching the process and went back to revise my manuscript. While I was willing to try this, I was also terrified at attempting something like this on my own. I didn't know anyone who had ever self-published and had no idea how to even go about it. After several weeks, I lost my momentum and walked away from the project. Maybe writing wasn't for me.

Several weeks later, I was invited to attend a ghost hunt at Parsonsfield Seminary, a place I'd always wanted to investigate. It was located in Maine, on the edge of the New Hampshire border and promised to be an interesting place to learn more about the paranormal world.

I had some hesitation about going though. The drive to Parsonsfield was over four hours long and I would have to drive it after working a full day of work. I would also have to arrange for someone to come in and care for my pets and would miss the lazy Saturday afternoon on the couch that I'd been fantasizing about all week long. Something in the back of my mind niggled at me though.

You need to go.

That was all I got. I didn't get a full-blown message filled with details about why I should go. I just got those four words. Thankfully, I listened to them and made the trek.

The investigation itself was interesting, but what happened the next morning was far more intriguing. It was the point in time when my life began to change in a dramatic way.

I met Barbara Williams the night before, but didn't get a chance to really talk with her. I knew she was a psychic medium who oversaw the investigations at Parsonsfield Seminary, but I found her to be a bit intimidating.

Barbara has a real presence about her. She is tall with long blond hair and has eyes that seem to peer right through you. She was the sort of woman who spoke her mind, not bothering to mince words or soft-pedal anything. She exuded confidence like some people radiate charm. It wafted off of her like an enchanting perfume, rich and intoxicating, but also more than a little daunting.

As we were leaving the following morning, she pulled me aside and asked if I would like a cleansing. As a devout student of the paranormal world, I was eager to experience this for the first time. I had no idea what her version of a cleansing would be like, but I was willing to put aside my fear in hopes I would learn something.

She began telling me about energy cords. They are invisible lines of energy that connect us to other people, locations and sometimes even to ghosts. She sat me in a chair and began snipping and pulling them off me.

Anyone who knows me, understands that I am a skeptic first. I often need to experience something before I will truly believe it. I had my reservations about these strange energy cords, but as she began removing them, I felt lighter. My exhaustion from a late night of investigating fell away, leaving me happy and eager for the day.

As she was finishing up, she asked me something that would change my life forever, right there on the spot.

"Have you just written a book?" she asked.

I nearly fell off my chair. My eyes must have looked like saucers as I turned to look at her. How could she possibly know that?

I told her about the last book I wrote, the one that I was close to giving up on. As I thought about it, some of the elation from the cleansing evaporated, leaving me feeling weak and powerless.

"You need to publish that as soon as possible. It will set off a chain of events that will launch your career," she told me, then added. "You're going to be so famous, I'm going to be able to say I knew you before you were."

Like many powerful mystics, she wouldn't tell me more. If I was hoping for blueprints and an outline of what I needed to do to reach my life-long goals, I wasn't going to get it.

I thanked her and hurried home, diving back into my book in true earnestness. I self-published the book less than two weeks after our conversation.

While that particular book didn't launch me into instant stardom, it did exactly what she said it would do: it started my writing career. Since that point in time, I went on to write thirteen more books, gaining more fans with each book.

Barbara also feels that my books will soon be made into movies, something that makes me jump up and down inside like a schoolgirl. She's since become one of my mentors, someone I can turn to when I have a question or a problem in the paranormal world. She's also become a friend, someone I trust with my life.

My publishing career has yet to launch me into super stardom. Truthfully, like many of you, I struggle to make ends meet. Barbara insures me that my time is coming soon and I believe her. After all, my loved ones sent her to me for a reason. I just have to trust that and be patient.

***

For Michelle Bate, the signs were so obvious she couldn't ignore them.

On her way to her mother's funeral, she had to stop for gas. When she went in to pay, she was surprised to see the clerk's nametag. Her name was Mary, which was also Michelle's mother's name. She thought it was interesting, but didn't think about it until she stopped for coffee. The woman who served her was also named Mary. Considering that Mary isn't as common of a name as it once was, she knew it was her mother sending her a sign that she was still with her, watching over her.

***

Other signs aren't as striking. Sometimes they come at unexpected times, breaking you out of the clutter of your mind to see them. Such was the case with Kathi Shultz.

One of her former clients would ask repeatedly about the tree outside her house, wanting to know what kind of tree it was. Kathi told her it was a chestnut tree and then began singing the Christmas Song to her.

"Chestnuts roasting on an open fire. Jack Frost nipping at your nose," she would say with a smile.

Her client passed away in the summer of 2015. In December, Kathi visited a local antique store for the first time. As she was walking through the store, perusing through the antiques, she passed a painting that caught her attention.

As she stopped to look at it, she caught her breath. It was an Andrew Wyeth print of "Chestnuts Roasting." With a smile and a tear in her eye, she immediately thought of her client. It was an amazing reminder that she was still thinking of her.

Signs come to everyone differently. If you are looking for one, pay attention to the details of your daily life and take notice of the things that stand out.

Chapter 6 - Scents

Lucinda Hester's mother loved flowers. She had a gardenia bush planted beside her front door and spent a lot of time caring for it. After her mother passed away, Lucinda often caught the scent of gardenias in places where there weren't any flowers and knew that it was a sign from her mother.

The first time she smelled it was on Mother's Day, a year after her mother passed. She was in the truck with several friends and everyone smelled it at the same time. They looked around, but didn't find any reason for the scent. It was just there and gone, long enough to be noted.

Another of her mother's favorite flowers was roses. During the Christmas season, Lucinda and her sister went to the hospital where her mother had spent time to put an ornament on the hospital's Christmas tree in honor of her. When they came home, something caught their attention. One single rose had bloomed on one of their mother's rose bushes. This was odd because it was in the middle of winter. Everything else surrounding it was dead and brown.

They felt it was her way of welcoming them home, almost as though she were standing at the door greeting them. Lucinda feels it was no coincidence that the rose that bloomed was pink since that was also her mother's favorite color.

(Above) Lucinda's sister behind the blooming rose

Loved ones often reveal their presence by sending us scents that we always associated with them. This makes perfect sense, considering scent has the strongest connection to memory recall than any of the other senses.

For some, the scent might be a favorite perfume or the smell of pipe tobacco. For others, it could be the aroma of a favorite meal or bread baking. Frequently, the smell is so faint and fleeting, you might attribute it to your imagination, but you shouldn't. It took a lot of energy for your loved one to send that to you. Appreciate it for the gift it was.

A man named Vladimir commented on my Ghost Diaries article with a story that is both comforting and sad at the same time.

After his wife passed away from cancer in 2003, he lost not only her, but the baby she was carrying. It was a devastating time for him, but he got through it as best as possible. Over the years since then, when he feels sad or angry, he often smells something that reminds him of her favorite perfume, something she only wore on special occasions.

When he first smelled it, it scared him because it was out of the realm of normal everyday life, but he's since learned to trust it as a sign that she is still looking after him. It now calms him down and allows him to carry on with his life.

***

For some people, the scent that they smell isn't very pleasant. After Laura Carr's grandfather passed away in 1991, the sign they received was enough to make them choke.

Her grandfather was always a heavy smoker. Soon after he passed away, the family began smelling cigarette smoke around them at odd times.

The first time Laura smelled it, she was perplexed. No one in the house smoked, so there wasn't a reason for the smell to be indoors, especially not so strong. She could understand if someone was walking past the house smoking and the stench drifted inside, but this smell was too strong for any rational explanations. It was almost as though someone was standing in the room with a lit cigarette.

Her mother saw her sniffing the air and asked her what she smelled.

"Cigarette smoke," Laura said.

"Yeah. Me too," her mother said, giving her a measured look. Laura's thoughts immediately turned to her grandfather, but she kept the information to herself.

Soon though, the smell happened so frequently, the family couldn't ignore it or pretend it wasn't there. They would smell it the strongest in her grandmother's room and began commenting on it, wondering if it was her grandfather.

At the time, they lived in Alabama, but in 2000, the entire family moved back to their home-state of Indiana. If they thought the smell would remain in Alabama, they were wrong. Two weeks after they moved back, they started smelling cigarette smoke there too.

Her grandmother fanned her face. "Looks like Eugene is here. He found me," she said.

Not long after they moved, her grandmother's health began to falter. She began to spend more time in her bedroom, confined to her bed. Not surprising, the family began smelling smoke in her room. The smell would come on strong and then disappear in an instant. It was like turning a switch on and off.

They also began hearing the sounds of doors slamming shut. It started getting creepy. If they at first thought that her grandpa was there to get her grandma and bring her to Heaven, they began to get worried it was something else altogether. Why would her grandpa slam doors?

In December of 2015, her grandmother grew ill enough to require hospitalization. Laura visited her at the hospital and was stunned when she walked in. The room absolutely reeked of cigarette smoke.

If she had any doubts that the smell was associated with her grandfather before, she quickly overcame them. No one was allowed to smoke within one thousand feet of the hospital.

"Grandpa's here," Laura said.

"I smell it too," her mother said, wrinkling her nose.

They eventually moved her grandmother to a nursing home and began smelling it there too.

It was clear that her grandmother's time was rapidly coming to an end. It was something everyone in the room could feel. Her grandmother had been sleeping for the better part of the week, but suddenly opened her eyes and looked around.

"What's happening to me?" she asked in a frail voice.

Her mother took her hand, feeling the tears brimming in her eyes. "It's okay. You can close your eyes and go to sleep."

"Grandpa is waiting for you," Laura added.

The smell of smoke suddenly grew even stronger. It was as though the entire room was filled with it. Then, her grandma took her last breath and passed quietly. At the moment she died, her mother saw Laura's grandfather standing beside her.

They left the hospital with heavy hearts. Her grandmother had been such a tremendous part of all their lives. Knowing she wasn't there any longer left her feeling empty and sad.

That night as she lay in bed trying to fall asleep, she heard a sound in the hallway. She got up and crept from her bedroom. Everything was in its place. The odor of cigarette smoke suddenly filled the hallway.

Her grandfather was there.

"What are you doing?" Laura asked nervously.

There was a long moment of silence, and then she heard her grandfather speak. "I'll only be a minute," he said.

She stood there, staring into the darkness until the smell of smoke faded.

Laura continues to experience signs that her grandfather is still around watching over them. Sometimes they smell cigarette smoke and doors have been known to open and close on their own in the house. She always thought her grandfather was there to comfort her grandmother, but now she wonders if he was there for all of them.

Skeptics might scoff at the notion, pointing out that cigarette smoke often finds its way into homes and automobiles. All you need to do is pass through someone's smoke and it gets pulled in through the vents. The same situation applies to smoke drifting in through opened windows, but Laura is a firm believer that the sign is as true as her grandfather's love for his family.

Recently, her parents got into their car to go grocery shopping. As soon as they pulled out of the driveway, the car filled with the stench of cigarette smoke. They looked around, not seeing anything that would contribute to the sudden smell. Instead, her father treated it with humor.

"Eugene, we don't smoke in the car!" her father said adamantly. The smell immediately dissipated.

***

In 2011, while Maria De Fatima was caring for her mother, who suffered from a long-term illness, she could feel her father's presence lingering nearby. It was as though he too was keeping a close eye on her mother. Since his death in 1993, he's given her many signs as a sign of his enduring love.

One night while she was with her mother, she woke up and smelled the scent of his cologne. The smell was so strong, she could even taste it. It was enough to make her look around the room, thinking someone had walked in while she was sitting there. After she checked out the rooms, satisfied that she was alone with her mother, she realized where the smell had come from.

Another time, she was crying and looked down to find a neatly folded white handkerchief. Her mother told her that it was a message from her father. When she lifted the handkerchief to her nose, she was amazed. It smelled just like her father.

Some people report smelling the scent of cough drops or menthol vapor cream, the kind that people often put on their chests when they feel congested.

While I was on a paranormal investigation, one of the investigators smelled cough drops. She asked around, thinking that someone on the team had a sore throat and was sucking on a lozenge, but no one was.

I remember pausing, trying to figure out where it came from, but there weren't any logical conclusions, so I just let it go. Now that I know what I do about spirit signs, I wish I would have asked her if someone she loved often used cough drops. It could have been a sign that was relative to her.

Others will smell the aroma of food cooking. When you smell something like this and can't find a logical explanation for it, go back to the first thought you had when you smelled it.

For years, the smell of rice cooking always reminded me of my grandmother Nanny. Since she was six when I died, I didn't understand the connection until I asked my mother. As it turns out, Nanny cooked a lot of rice. When I smell it at odd times, it reminds me that she's still here with me, watching over me.

Chapter 7 - Dreams

When we sleep, our vibration rises, nearly matching the higher vibration of loved ones in spirit form. Because our subconscious minds are far less cluttered than our waking minds, spirits have an easier time getting through to us.

For many, dreams of this nature have a realistic texture to them, not feeling as dreamlike as most dreams. These dreams might be more colorful or filled with details you wouldn't normally see. They don't have the usual tendency to stray off into strange settings and seem more like a memory than a dream.

You will also have a higher probability of remembering it, even if you don't normally remember your dreams. It won't fade to dust the moment your feet hit the floor in the morning. You will think about this dream all day long, pondering over it.

When you have dreams of this nature, pay close attention to them. They might be a message from beyond the grave.

Gare Allen, the author of *The Dead,* an account of his paranormal and metaphysical experiences, shares a story about his mother who passed away in 2014.

Gare's Story

On a Sunday night in mid-July of 2009, I went to bed a little after eleven o'clock. Sometime during my slumber, I had a disturbing dream about my mother.

I dreamed that she was in my living room and I was on the other side of the house. She was trying to get my attention but I was busy with other people. I finally got free and walked over to her. She took me outside and pointed to the top of the front bedroom. With a terrified expression, she told me, "He is trying to get me." Suddenly, her image shook and became distorted, almost like a hologram that was losing its projection.

My blackberry phone automatically turned off at eleven o'clock p.m. and turned back on at seven o'clock a.m. I wouldn't know if I had received a phone call during that time period until the next morning. I woke up at seven-thirty and found that I had a voice mail.

The message was from my mother. She woke up in the middle of the night with severe chest pains and informed me that she planned on calling 911. I called her cell and home line, but there was no answer.

Immediately, and in a panic, I drove to her house expecting the worst. She wasn't home. I quickly found out that she had called 911 and was stabilized in a nearby hospital, after having suffered a heart attack.

In the coming week, she would undergo heart surgery, spend two weeks in the hospital in recovery and then be released and stay with me.

A week into her continued recovery at my home, she began to have mini seizures. She would lose the time and not remember anything while she was seizing. Afterward, she would be disoriented and understandably agitated.

On the evening of August 9th, 2009, I helped my mother into bed and she immediately had a short, mini seizure. However, this time, when she came out of it, she was smiling and appeared tranquil and calm. My mother looked at me with a loving smile and spoke evenly in a soothing tone and told me, "It's alright, now. You're a good son and I love you."

Her words, while loving and kind, set off an alarm in my heart. It sounded too much like a goodbye. I tried to watch television, but after a few minutes I went back to check in on her and found her sleeping. After waiting another thirty minutes or so, I noticed that my foot had been, involuntarily, tapping the ground.

Anxious, I returned to the bedroom. Without turning on the light, I knew she had passed.

The room was filled with an overwhelming sense of peace.

Suddenly, without warning, the palpable warm, tranquility vanished and secular reality punched me in the heart.

I had lost my mother.

From that point forward, I had hundreds of dreams of my mother. The first, and most precious to me, occurred just two days after her passing.

In the dream, we were standing in the kitchen of the house in which I spent the majority of my childhood. I asked her how she was doing. She replied that she was still having trouble regulating her blood pressure.

I somehow understood in the dream that she had still possessed aspects of her physical body after passing. My mom had high blood pressure for the majority of her life and it had remained even after death. At least, in this dream.

We moved to the driveway where I helped my mother into a convertible car, with the top down. I then placed her cat in a carrier and secured it in the backseat. After handing her a plate of food, she began to drive off down the road.

I watched her drive off only to see her stop and return so that I could put the top up.

I had a convertible in my twenties and while she loved riding in it, the older adult in her would worry about the state of her hair in the whipping wind.

After putting the top up, she drove off and out of sight.

When I woke from this wonderful dream, I felt like I had taken care of her, even after she passed.

My mother had grown up near the water and often told me of the days that she would enjoy driving along the beaches with the convertible top down on her car.

During my childhood, we made frequent trips to the beach. Her favorite water spot was Ft. DeSoto Beach, which is where I spread her ashes.

I recall the drive to Ft. Desoto Beach after her memorial. I asked my spirit guide for a pod of dolphins as a way of honoring my mother. I was more than grateful to see that when my brothers and I spread her ashes into the ocean, not one, but two pods of dolphins swam and jumped through the waves, just yards from us.

I still had one more thing to do and that was finding a home for my mother's cat.

Due to the canine hierarchy that ruled my home, I was unable to care for her feline companion. After weeks of searching for a home for her, I connected with an employee at my company, named Tonya. She told me that she managed a small cat rescue on her farm and would be willing to take my mom's former companion animal.

The cat was grumpy and, in my mother's estimation anyway, just *slightly* overweight. Regardless, it appeared that the feisty feline still had some life in front of her so I transferred custody.

A few weeks later, I was giving a presentation where Tonya was in attendance. During lunch, she happened to sit at my table with several other associates.

Without being asked, she blurts out, "Your mom's cat died."

I was dumfounded and just stared at her.

She continued. "I was sleeping on the couch the next day and as I woke up, someone whispered in my ear, 'Thank you for taking care of my cat.'"

Then, she got up and left the table. The other people, one by one, left as well until I was sitting alone trying to reconcile what Tonya had just told me. I felt like I had lost my mother all over again.

Somehow, I managed to conduct the remainder of my presentation, but I don't recall much of it.

That night, I dreamt of my mother. We were sitting on a front porch step and she was telling me that she was going to be reborn as a girl in Greensboro, North Carolina. After our chat, she said she had to leave. I watched her drive down a highway.

I awoke, knowing that my mother was going to be alright.

In this, and countless other dreams of my mother, she would never look at me. Her eyes would either be blurred out or she would not be facing me.

At first, I took this as concerning symbolism but then I recalled a phone call we received just hours after my mother passed. She had signed up to be an organ donor and they wanted permission to remove her eyes.

Once I remembered this, I would see her eyes in my dreams.

The first Mother's Day after her passing was especially difficult. To honor her, I ate at her favorite restaurant. As the server approached the table I noted the name tag displaying the name Victoria, my mother's name. I instantly felt my mother's presence and silently sent my love to her.

A year or so later I was still missing my mother terribly. I knew in my heart that she was at peace but still longed for another sign of her presence.

One afternoon I stood in my kitchen and began to dictate a text using the voice option. I pressed the record button but it quickly turned itself off. Without having said a word and with no background noise, the text read, "Mom good." A wide beaming smile accompanied my happy tears.

***

Some dreams seem to have a sense of prophesy to them. A year after Lucinda Hester's mother passed away, she had a dream about her mother. In the dream, she was at her mother's house, sitting on her couch. Her mother was sitting beside her, holding a two year old boy. Instinctively, Lucinda knew that the baby was her grandson.

She woke up the next morning feeling as though she'd been given a gift. The dream was so realistic, she felt like she was looking at a snapshot of the future.

Her daughter was pregnant, but they didn't yet know the sex of the child. Was it going to be a boy? Had her mother sent her this image?

Three years later, she looks back with amazement. Not only did her grandchild end up being a boy, but he looks and acts exactly like the child she dreamed about so long ago.

***

Many people yearn for some sort of confirmation, only to find their yearnings unfulfilled. Such was the case with Laura Pelletier.

Her mother passed away in 2009. Despite her pleas to her mother to come to her in a dream, she had minimal experiences. Sometimes her mother would be in a dream, but it felt more like a normal dream than a communicative one.

After I posted a message online, asking for people's experiences with communicating with passed on loved ones, Laura messaged me. After seven long years of not getting the communication she longed for, she finally had a dream that felt real.

In the dream, she asked her brother where her mother was. He told her that she was at the 99 Restaurant in Methuen, Massachusetts, having a drink with Rich.

Rich had been a close friend of her mothers who had also passed away. It made perfect sense to Laura that her mother would be having a drink with him in her favorite restaurant. While it wasn't the direct communication she had hoped for, she knew that the message was real. Her mother was safe and happy, having a drink with an old friend in a comfortable location.

***

Suzanne Lynch's experience with dreams meant the difference between life and death for her son.

Suzanne's son was stationed in Afghanistan. One night he had a dream about his grandmother and his cousin. They both died within the same year when he was only six years old, so his memories of them were vague, at best. He thought it was strange that he would be dreaming about them, but even more perplexing was the message they gave him.

"Be careful of the hill," they told him just before he woke up.

The area he was stationed in often saw a large amount of gunfire, so he was careful no matter where he was. He just kept his eyes open more carefully, especially when he was on top of any hills.

One day, he mentioned the dream to one of his buddies. The man was shocked.

"You're not going to believe this, but my girlfriend had the same dream and said the same thing. She said she saw something bad happening on a hill and to be careful of any hills," his friend told him.

It seemed too coincidental that two separate people would have the same dream. He wouldn't learn what it meant until several days later when he was almost hit by a bullet.

It came so close to him, he felt it zip through the air beside his ear. One inch closer and he would have been killed. The most striking thing about the incident was the location. He was standing on a hill when it happened.

The dream would stay with him and his mother for a lifetime.

***

Jennifer also had a dream that felt more like a message.

Two years after her grandfather died, Jennifer was sleeping at her grandmother's house when she had an interesting dream. In the dream, her grandfather walked into the house, went directly to the refrigerator before sitting down at the table. Everyone in the house froze like statues except for her two daughters.

She asked him what he was doing there because he was supposed to be dead. He told her that he knew he was dead. He had been in a place that was similar to jail because he had done something wrong, but he was now allowed to eat and go fishing again.

It was one of the most realistic dreams Jennifer has ever had and she knew it was more than just a dream. Her grandfather was communicating with her. It helped her develop a new calmness about the other side.

***

A woman I will call Kathy shared the following story.

Kathy's story

From a small child till present I have been able to see, hear and feel things that others couldn't.

For a period I was afraid to sleep in fear that I might have a bad dream. My dreams were coming true the very next day. Three separate occasions, I dreamed of being at a family member's funeral, while none were expected to pass. I would receive a phone call in the morning that they had.

Simple silly dreams would also come true the very next day, like boxes falling of a delivery truck in front of my house, and so on. I often have feelings to call and check on someone only to find out they are sick or hurt.

My son now has these overwhelming feelings too and will call. Since my mother passed, so many things have happened to let me know she is with me. She knew of these "happenings"

During one of our last conversations, she promised that she would let me know she was with me. Several things have happened to let me know she is here, but the most noted is the number 222 I see very often without looking for it.

I'm a nurse and took care of her till she passed. One pain medication (Morphine) she knew she could have every two hours but couldn't say the name of, so she would say 222 and I knew what she wanted. The smells, the quick glance that I saw something I have it all. Thank you for taking the time to read this.

***

On the night that David Cadmus's mother passed away, she came to him in a dream. She told him that everything was going to be okay. She was wearing the same dress she ended up being buried in. When he woke up, he discovered that her sisters were bringing that same dress to the funeral home.

Seeing the dress in his dream before witnessing it in real life made him realize that it was more than a dream. It was his mother's way of saying goodbye to him.

***

One friend who asked to remain anonymous shared a story with me that gave me chills. I changed her name to preserve her identity.

Danielle was the youngest of four siblings. When she was born, her sister Debbie was ten, and her two brothers, Andy and Sam were eight and nine.

The siblings didn't always get along, but most of it was due to one of her brothers. She couldn't explain it, but Andy had a definite mean streak to him. The only person in the family he was capable of getting along with was Danielle's sister, Debbie.

"She could deal with Andy back then and Sam and I were inseparable. It was as if we both had our own brother. I had Sam and she had Andy."

She was always very close to Sam while they were growing up. "Sam never called me by name. I was baby girl or baby sister. He was extremely protective of me. On more than one occasion, he and Andy got in a fist fight over Andy freaking out and trying to attack me," she said.

Andy seemed to always hate Danielle, no matter what she did or didn't do. Her parents thought it was because he was the baby of the family until she was born and she took some of the attention away from him.

"He has no problem using violence and is a master at emotional abuse. I avoid him like he's the devil himself," she added.

The family lived in New Orleans when Hurricane Katrina hit. They ended up evacuating to Mississippi, which was close to where Sam was living. When the family got the "all clear" to go home, Sam wanted to come help them rebuild but Andy threw a fit and didn't want him there. In the end Sam didn't go, something that made Danielle sad.

"We all moved into a small one bedroom apartment while we rebuilt our homes. It was horrible. You had to tiptoe around and try to stay invisible when Andy was around. Luckily he usually stayed at my mom's house which he was rebuilding," she said.

In January, the family received some devastating news. Sam had been murdered.

"I can't begin to explain the heartbreak," Danielle said. "One night Andy was there and had one of his fits. I actually was in full on panic mode trying to keep him from attacking me, my two kids or my mom. I'm standing there unsure what to do when I heard Sam telling me, "It's ok baby girl. You got this. Quietly get mom and y'all take a ride,"

Danielle was astounded by the words. She turned her head and looked around the room, fully expecting to see her brother standing there, but the room was empty. The words sounded as clear as though they were spoken by a living person. They were enough to jump start her into action.

She felt a sense of calmness come over her and was successfully able to get everyone out of the house without arousing Andy's suspicions. When they got back to the house, Andy was gone.

It happened three more times before their homes were finally finished. Once they moved out of her mother's house and away from Andy, the communication with Sam came to a halt.

Years later, Danielle had a dream about her deceased father that surprised her. In the dream, she was riding in a truck with her father.

"It was like I was a teenager again and he was picking me up to bring me home one evening. We were riding in truck and talking," she said. Then, her father was gone and her husband was in his place.

When she told me about her dream, I wondered about the symbolism of the truck. Because her husband drives trucks for a living, was she making the connection that her father made her feel safe just like her husband does now?

She nearly cried when I asked her that.

"That's one of the things that's always bothered me is knowing if Dad approved. I wanted him to let me know if I can finally actually let my guard down and truly trust again," she said.

The timing of the dream was also relevant. It happened a week after the anniversary of Sam's death.

"I told my husband that I'm so lost because my dad and brother were my strength. I knew there wasn't anything I needed to be afraid of with them around. They'd always be there and I knew there wasn't anything I could ever do to change how they felt about me," she said.

Her husband looked at her with a small smile and told her that she needed to look to him for that now, making the symbolism in the dream even more relevant.

***

Leslie Cuebeans has had quite a few strange dreams about her mother since she passed away in September of 2013. She notices that her mother seems to come to her in dreams when Leslie misses her the most.

Unlike many others, she's had an easy time reaching her mother in dreams. When she asked her to come to her, her mother nearly always complied.

In the majority of her dreams, her mother was with her father, traveling to other places, which was strange because her father was still alive. They were always in a rush to get somewhere.

One dream was remarkably similar to a real life event. In the dream, Leslie had a car accident and her mother was there. In real life, her mother and father were in a near-fatal car accident together, which they somehow survived. In the dream, the car was totaled, but Leslie managed to walk away unscathed. She believes it's a sign from her mother to get over the way she felt when they were in the accident.

She knew the last dream she had of her would be the last one while she was having it. In the dream, there was a stretcher waiting for her mother and she was supposed to die again.

In the dream, her mother wasn't happy about having to die again, but she also knew she didn't have a choice. Since she was rushed, she didn't have time to really talk to Leslie. Leslie just remembers leaning over the empty stretcher, crying because she wanted to have more time with her.

As it turns out, her mother had one more sign to give her. One day, the smell of cigarette smoke filled her car. She really hated the smell because she had quit smoking years ago and the smell bothered her.

"Oh my God, that smells gross! Go away!" she said aloud and the smell immediately vanished.

She's fairly certain the smell was from her mother. She used to hate it as a child when her mother came up to kiss her goodnight right after smoking a cigarette. Even though she was disgusted by the smell, she's glad that her mother made the effort to let her know she was okay and still looking over her.

***

Shawn Todd also shared a personal, but touching story with me.

Many years ago, he was engaged. His fiancé was killed in an accident, but he didn't find out about it until the next day. The night she died, he had a dream about her.

In the dream, he was floating above a beautiful park setting. There were many happy people there who were dressed in white clothing, having picnics and playing games. It reminded him of the painting *Sunday in the Park* by George Seurat.

He zoomed in on a girl in the dream who was dressed in a white sundress. She was sitting alone in the middle of the park. As he was looking at her, she turned around and he realized it was his fiancé. With a slight smile, she told him that she would always love him and that she would be waiting for him. He was awoken from the dream by a phone call from her father, telling him about her accident.

After reading his story, it became even clearer to me that love survives death. Of all emotions, love has the highest vibration, something that transcends our physical barriers.

***

Crystal Pina comes to my Paranormal 101 class and has become a close personal friend. I was pleased when she offered to share a story with me.

Years ago, after her aunt's boyfriend passed away from cancer, she went to stay with her aunt to help her with funeral arrangements and to offer her some measure of comfort.

One night while she was there, she had a dream about him. In the dream, he was wearing a red sweat suit. When she woke up, she found the dream to be bizarre. Her aunt's boyfriend would have never have worn a sweat suit, never mind a red one.

The next morning, she told her aunt about her dream and they couldn't make any sense of it. Her aunt couldn't imagine him wearing anything like that either. He was more of a jeans and t-shirt kind of guy. The conversation faded as they began looking through his closet to search for an outfit for him to be buried in.

He was very much into Chinese decorations. He had a lot of dishes and wall hangings with Chinese patterns and pictures on them. They ended up finding a black shirt with a big red Chinese dragon on the back. As soon as she saw it, she realized the red dragon symbolizes the red sweatshirt and knew that was what he should be buried in.

In Crystal's example, it is sometimes difficult for loved ones to come through in dreams because they have to part through our normal dream-state to get their message through. They will often use symbolism to let us understand what they are saying. Crystal knew that the red sweat suit wasn't right, but understood the message as soon as she saw the red dragon.

***

Charles Reis is a fellow paranormal investigator and the co-founder of *Creepy Places in New England,* a documentary styled show that airs on YouTube. Charles and his friend Stephen Moreau document haunted locations all around New England and films their experiences. I've had the pleasure of being on two of their shows and found the process intriguing. Below is a clip of their show about the S.K. Pierce Haunted Victorian Mansion.

https://www.youtube.com/watch?v=UwMhbPdg1vc

Charles' story

Back in 2003, my dad (Charles Sr.) was hugely overweight. To lose weight, he got that gastro-bypass surgery. After the surgery he was fine, but I was told about an hour later, he knew something was wrong.

His body started to shut down and he slipped into a coma. There was some type of infection that slowly shut down his body, so they pumped him full of some medication to keep his heart going. Unfortunately, it sucked the oxygen out of his brain, leaving him brain dead.

My mom had to make the decision (with help from her sisters) to end the medication, which would cause his heart to stop. Me and my sisters (my younger brother and sister were too young and weren't there) got some alone time and got to say goodbye.

I did my time with him even though I already knew he was gone. Afterwards, the room at the hospital was filled with my father's friends and family.

After almost an hour, we watched as the heart rate slowed, until it went flat lined (took like about 20 to 25 minutes for the heart to slow down and stop).

My mother broke down, and after a lot of crying, I went home with her to Coventry and stayed the night (I was living in Providence at the time).

I was sleeping in the spare room in the basement, I couldn't sleep but I did fall asleep around 3am. I had a weird dream of my father dying in bed. Then, after my family placed the cover over him, we took it off and in his place was a baby. I woke up from that dream.

When I looked to my right I saw my father staring at me. He looked completely solid, as if there really was a person standing next to me. I remembered his face well, it showed sadness, and I got the idea that my father was sad, not necessarily for dying, but for having to leave the family with some things left unresolved, especially since he and I had a strenuous relationship. And his death left it unresolved and we never had a chance to make peace, but in a way, him showing himself to me that night was a way of me moving on and making peace with the past.

Like several other stories, Charles' dream was filled with symbolism. According to dream experts, seeing a baby in your dreams could point to several subconscious messages. It could symbolize innocence or vulnerability, but in Charles' case, the message was clear. His father was reborn and was in a place where he felt safe and nurtured. It was a nice message for Charles to receive.

***

Robin Gootee McDowell is another paranormal investigator friend who lives in southern Indiana. I met her through our parents, who frequent the same social club, and ended up going on several investigations with her while I was visiting family in Indiana.

Robin's Story

I have a story that has always held a special place in my heart. In 1987 I lost a little boy that I named Anthony.

In Sept of 1996 one of my dearest friends lost a little boy named Cody. The night after she delivered Cody, I had a dream/vision (not sure what to call it.) I saw two little boys. One was a few years older than the other.

I knew that one was my Anthony. He had fire-engine red hair and looked just like my husband. The other I knew was Cody. He had sandy-brown hair and looked just like his mom.

Anthony and Cody (don't ask why I knew I just knew these were our sons) were holding hands and running through a field of corn flowers and butterflies. I could hear the birds. It's funny that after all these years the details are still as fresh as the day it happened.

The two boys turned to look at me as if to say, "Hey, we got this. We're okay."

I didn't tell Shannon until about a week later when she came to see me. Shannon and I were talking and she pulled out some pictures of Cody and I could not believe my eyes. The little boy in the pictures was the same one in my dream/vision. This only confirmed what I had seen. When I told her we sat and laughed through tears that our boys would be together in death as we are in life.

It was a long healing process for both of us. Shannon knew that Cody was most likely not going to live past birth. He had abdominal developmental disorder and there was little past prayer that could be done, so she left it in God's hands. We spent many hours before his birth talking praying and crying. I told her to make sure to hold him and love him before she let them take Cody from her. That is something that had haunted me for years after I lost Anthony. I was not able to hold him or see him or bury him. Back then they didn't allow for such things. I was at the beginning of my 2nd trimester when I lost him. So in his own way Cody was my healing and Anthony and I were Shannon's healing.

***

As a paranormal investigator, stories from other investigators always intrigue me. There is so much we don't know about the paranormal world. Connecting with someone in spirit form is often the best way to find out.

When Dawn Mooney, founder of Gateway of Shadows Paranormal Investigations from Edwardsville, Illinois contacted me with a story, I was eager to read it.

Growing up, Dawn's uncle Kevin was her hands-down favorite. He was only seven years older than her and was the coolest person she knew.

When she was fifteen years-old, her entire family was gathered for Thanksgiving at her parent's house. The only person who was missing was her Uncle Kevin. Instead of having dinner with the family, he decided to go duck hunting on that cold, misty, rainy day instead.

Her mother and grandmother were finishing up the preparations, while her grandfather was downstairs watching television. Her father wandered through the kitchen, looking for a pre-dinner snack as the house filled with the delicious aroma of the Thanksgiving feast.

Dawn ran upstairs to get something when the phone rang. Since her father worked for the phone company, she had her own "teen line" in her bedroom. When she picked up the phone, an unfamiliar voice was on the other end of the line.

"Do you have a relative by the name of Kevin _____?" he asked.

"Yes," she answered hesitantly.

Without asking how old she was, he went on to tell her that Kevin had drowned that morning in Rend Lake.

Her entire world crashed down around her in that moment. Just a week earlier, her Uncle Kevin had promised to take her to her first concert soon. Memories flooded her mind in a torrent, but she knew she had to hold it all together for the sake of her family.

"Let me go get my dad," she told the caller and ran for the stairs.

She tried hard to keep her emotions in check so she wouldn't alert her grandparents, who were Kevin's mother and father. As she got to the top of the stairs, her father appeared at the bottom landing, almost as though he knew something had happened.

"Kevin drowned!" she mouthed to him.

He looked at her with shock in his eyes. "What?"

"Kevin drowned!" she said again. This time her words hit their mark.

"Oh no! Oh my God!" he said and ran to get her grandfather on the line. It was a moment that would forever be frozen in time in her mind. Kevin was only twenty-two years-old.

(Above) Dawn's Uncle Kevin

Despite the tragic loss, life went on, as it always does. Dawn graduated from high school two years later, got married, had two beautiful daughters and eventually got divorced. Memories of her Uncle Kevin never left her though. She thought about him often.

In 2006, on a weekend that her girls were visiting their father, Dawn sat in her living room with her boyfriend watching television. As she sat there, she suddenly began feeling something moving in her hair.

She asked her boyfriend if she had a bug in her hair, but he couldn't find anything. The feeling simply wouldn't go away. She asked him several more times, to the point where he began getting aggravated, but no bug could be found.

When she went to bed that night, she had a dream that made her wonder if it wasn't a bug, but something else altogether.

In the dream, she was standing in her kitchen. She could hear a voice speaking to her. It seemed to come from everywhere. Even when she turned, she could hear it, but couldn't find the source of the voice. All she knew was that it was female.

"You need to go outside. There is someone waiting for you," the voice said.

She hesitated, not knowing what to do. "Who is it?" she asked, but the voice wouldn't tell her.

"You will see when you go outside," was all it would say.

"Fine!" she said and walked to the back door, which opened up to a short flight of stairs that led to the carport. She walked out to the stoop and looked to her right. There, she saw a man.

"Can I help you?" she asked.

He said, "You don't recognize me do you?"

"No, I'm sorry. You look really familiar but I can't place you," she told him.

"It's Kevin," he said, nearly sending her to her knees. "Come with me I want to show you something."

The next thing she knew, they were hovering above the lake where he drowned. Even though the sensation was strange, she wasn't afraid.

She could see something in the water below them. As she stared, trying to make them out, she realized they were gray, smoky figures that looked like statues. She asked him what they were and he told her that they were all the others who had drowned in the lake. She felt a sense of sadness wash over her. The shock of seeing them nearly overwhelming.

Without having a sense of traveling, they were suddenly on a grassy hill beside the lake. He asked her if she had any questions for him.

Being a paranormal investigator, her curiosity was piqued. Even though she wasn't investigating full time, she had been on enough investigations that she knew the one question she wanted to ask.

"Why is it that when some spirits talk they sound all muffled or garbled?"

"I'll show you," he said.

All of a sudden, her head tilted back and her mouth opened. A substance that felt like water fell down from the sky and went into her body. He then asked her to try to talk, but when she did, her words were garbled as though she were attempting to talk while under water.

Then just as quickly as it started, her head tilted back again and the water left her body.

"Do you understand?" he asked.

She thought she did, but she asked him to repeat it one more time until it truly sunk in. After the second time, she nodded and told him she understood.

"I just wanted you to know that I am happy and doing fine," he told her.

She looked at him and smiled, then sat straight up in her bed, coming out of the dream in an instant. Tears streamed down her cheeks as she thought about it. It was the most amazing experience she'd ever had. She'd never forget it.

After the dream, Dawn had several other encounters that made her wonder if Kevin was still hanging around. Sometimes the broken doorbell would start ringing randomly. When she met her current husband, he didn't believe her until she made it ring on command.

"That incident gave me a little piece of mind and allowed me to deal with his death a little better. I was finally able, after twenty-five years to visit his gravesite. Twenty-five years to the day! How that happened is another story for another day. Spirit is amazing!" Dawn said.

I often ask my spirit guides and deceased loved ones to come to me in dreams to help me figure out difficult parts of my life. As long as it doesn't interfere with my life plan, I've had quite a bit of success with this.

Recently, I had an experience that seemed more real than dreamlike.

My son and I have been sharing an apartment while he goes to college. This worked out for over two years, but the time has come for us to go our separate ways. He is eager to move in with his long-term girlfriend and I would like to be closer to where my friends live.

I grew stressed trying to figure out where I should go. The town I wanted to live in was too expensive and the places I could afford were too far away.

"Please show me in a dream," I pleaded right before I went to bed.

That night, I had a very clear dream of where I should move. It was present to me in a way that made me see that being there wouldn't be as bad as I originally thought it would be. All I had to do was get over my initial concerns and look for the positive aspects, instead of focusing on the negative.

Many people have had success with this, so give it a try. If you're taking sleep medications, this might hamper your dreams, as well as your memory of them.

If you do have a dream of this nature, write it down as soon as you wake up, recording every possible detail you can recall. Dreams often fade away quickly, since they aren't recorded in our memory banks. The part of the brain that processes memories is deactivated while we sleep, so we have to be diligent upon waking to pull all the information we can from them.

If your loved one comes to you in a dream, cherish it, even if it's not exactly what you hoped for. Sometimes the dream itself is symbolic and will mean something different to you after you give it some thought.

Chapter 8 – Pennies from Heaven

*O*ur loved ones come to us in a variety of ways. One method is by leaving coins. Some people might roll their eyes at the idea, but people who have received these gifts know better.

According to Barbara Williams, even if people recognize the signs, they don't often tell anyone.

"People don't talk about a lot of these things because they don't want to sound crazy. If you don't have someone around who is comfortable talking about it you may not bring that up," she said.

"You have to understand that signs of that nature come from loved ones as well as from the angelic realm. It will come from wherever there is support for that person," she added.

This means that signs like pennies from Heaven could also be coming from your spirit guides or from the angels who look over you.

***

Suzie Mendonca Dennehy's story has many layers. Separately, they are interesting stories, but when they are put together, they paint a much larger picture.

When Suzie was in high school, she was friends with a girl named Colleen who was a fellow cheerleader. Colleen was outgoing and pretty, popular with all her peers. When she died unexpectedly from a congenital heart defect at a cheerleading competition, Suzie and all her friends were devastated.

After her death, Suzie couldn't help but remember the events from the day before. They spent the entire afternoon practicing their maneuvers, over and over again. By the end of the day, everyone was getting a bit slap happy, especially Colleen.

She had a small yellow duck in her hand and started squeaking it. Every time someone would protest, she would squeak it again, garnering laughs from her friends.

"Give it a break, Colleen!" someone said.

Colleen squeaked it again with a smile.

Suzie knew she'd never get the duck away from her friend, so she ran over and grabbed the bouquet of daffodils that Colleen had purchased earlier in the day at a fundraising event.

"Hey! Bring those back!" Colleen called.

With a grin, Suzie gave them to a guy who was considered the class clown. He took a bite out of them, making everyone laugh. It was a moment in time that Suzie would never forget, highlighting the amicable nature of her group.

The next day, after Colleen's sudden death, Suzie found herself too overwhelmed to remain in the room with everyone. As she walked into another room, she inadvertently stepped on the yellow duck that Colleen had been squeaking just the day before. She smiled and shook her head, but picked it up nonetheless. She still has it to this day.

Twenty years later, she was at an intersection in nearby Acton, Massachusetts, and saw a truck drive past with Colleen's name on it. Her parents had contributed to a local TV station in her honor. It made Suzie think about the yellow squeaky duck. She called a friend who was there that day and asked her if she thought that Colleen's brother would like to have the duck.

The friend didn't think he'd want it. Even though twenty years had passed, the family was still very much in mourning. Suzie wondered if she should bring the duck to Colleen's grave instead. It just felt wrong hanging onto it. She decided to let the Universe decide.

"If I should bring the duck to her grave, show me a red truck. If I shouldn't bring it to her grave, show me a blue truck," she said, watching for the signs. Within five minutes, her friend Donna texted her.

"Suzie, this is going to sound strange, but does the color blue mean anything to you today?" she asked.

Suzie smiled. It wasn't the blue or red truck she had asked for, but it was enough confirmation for her. She kept the duck and brought a bouquet of daffodils to Colleen's grave instead.

Years later, after Suzie had her own children, she received confirmation that Colleen was still with her.

Suzie's son Jack lost a tooth. Instead of telling his mother about it, he placed it under his pillow to test the Tooth Fairy theory.

The next morning, he was excited. There was thirty-four cents under his pillow and the tooth was gone.

Suzie was fairly astounded. Since no one else in the house even knew about his missing tooth, there wasn't a logical explanation for the sudden appearance of the money.

Later that day, she went to the cemetery to visit Colleen's grave and was shocked by what she saw. Lined up on top of the grave was exactly thirty-four cents, the same amount left under her son's pillow the night before.

I asked Suzie if there was any relevance to the number thirty-four. According to the Angel Numbers, the number thirty-four means that her Ascended Masters and spiritual advisors were nearby, encouraging her to communicate with her, but she didn't think that was the message.

When she first began to get insight into the metaphysical world, she came across a website called *Thee Trinity Creation*. She felt prompted to study sacred geometry and numerology. The page taught her that thirty-four meant happiness.

If Colleen did indeed place the thirty-four cents under Suzie's son's pillow, it meant that she has been with Suzie for most of her life, cheering her on from the other side. Regardless, Suzie found the message to be comforting. She'll never forget her friendship with Colleen and will do her best to always honor her memory, which includes making her own life the happiest it can possibly be.

***

Leslie Cuebeans often finds dimes when she finds herself thinking of her mother who passed away.

"I find them in driveways and every house I visit. Once I found one in the kitchen, in the middle of the floor," she said.

Donna also receives coins as signs. After her mother passed away, she often finds a quarter when she finds herself thinking about her mother.

Her first quarter came at an unlikely moment: when she was doing laundry.

She was always careful to check all the pockets before putting them in the washing machine, so she was surprised to hear the sound of a coin banging around in the dryer once she switched the load over.

She opened the dryer and found a quarter. This was odd to her because the load of laundry contained mostly night clothes and towels. She pulled the quarter out and marveled at it, wondering if her mother was sending her a message.

She turned it back on again and heard the sound of more money tumbling with the laundry. When she opened the dryer door, she found another quarter.

It made her smile. "Okay, Mom. I heard you loud and clear. When I find a quarter, I'll know you are talking to me," she said. It was ironic to her that her mother chose laundry day to send a message. Her mother always hated the way she did laundry.

Since then, she's had many other instances where quarters show up in unexpected places. When she finds one, she smiles knowing that her mother would never send anything as paltry as a penny. She'd only send silver in the form of a quarter.

***

For Carla, the sign was dimes.

She wasn't someone who took much stock in the paranormal until she began getting signs from beyond the grave.

After her mother-in-law passed away, her husband began finding dimes in unusual places. They looked it up online and discovered that it could be a sign that his mother was letting them know she was still nearby. Her husband kept all the dimes, treasuring them. She wouldn't realize how pertinent the sign was until her husband too passed away.

Soon after his death, she began finding more dimes. This time, the occurrences weren't random. She always found the dimes in specific places that meant something to her, at times when she needed the signs the most. It was clear to her that her husband was sending them, just like his mother had done before him.

When people find coins, I always recommend that they check the date on the coin. Sometimes our loved ones will send us a coin with a specific year on it that marked a certain milestone in our life.

For others, the sign could be heads versus tails.

***

After Janine Clark's mother passed away five years ago from diverticulitis, she was two-thousand miles away and couldn't be there for her passing. It was heartbreaking for Janine because her mother had always been her rock.

Sometime later, she visited a well-known psychic in Florida in hopes of communicating with her mother. The psychic told her things that only her mother would know. Upon leaving, Janine asked the psychic how she would know her mother was around.

"Dimes!" she said. "And they have to be tails up. You'll see them when she visits."

It prompted a memory for Janine. She remembered seeing a dime sitting on her kitchen window sill. She didn't think much about it at the time. It had been there for several months, seemingly appearing out of nowhere.

When she got home from visiting the psychic, she went straight to her kitchen to look for it. It was tails up, as promised.

A friend of hers made her a bracelet and put the dime in the center of it as a remembrance. *(See photo left).*

Since that first dime, she has since found many more and they are always tails up. She has her mother's ashes near her bed, along with her rosary and picture.

One day, while she was cleaning, she was amazed at what she found. There was a dime sitting right in front of her ashes and it was once again tails up. She finds the messages comforting, knowing her mother is still around watching over her and her father.

***

Tony Woodland's first brush with the paranormal world came when he was just a teenager. I know Tony personally and was interested in hearing this story. Tony sought me out in 2015 after experiencing an extreme haunting in his house, a story I later documented in my book *Ruin of Souls*.

He was thirteen years-old when his mother's long-term live-in boyfriend Jim died from throat cancer, caused by smoking and drinking. A few months later, they saw the first signs of Jim's lingering presence.

On Christmas Eve of that year, Tony was reclining on the couch watching football. His two young nephews were over and were keeping themselves entertained by playing around the house. His mother was in the kitchen, working on meal preparations. Otherwise, it was a normal night in the Woodland household.

When Jim was alive, he loved to sit in his rocking chair in the kitchen by the window. Out of respect for his memory, they didn't remove the chair after his death, always thinking of it as "Jim's chair." With so many people coming over for the holidays though, they needed to temporarily relocate it. Tony's mother asked him to move it to her bedroom to make more space.

"Jim's not going to be happy about this," Tony's mother joked as he moved the chair. Tony didn't think much about it until hours later when he reclined on the couch watching TV.

Tony had a clear view of his mother's bedroom from the couch through the glass French doors that separated the space. Out of the corner of his eye, he swore he saw the chair move in her bedroom. He dismissed it as imagination until it happened again.

Out of curiosity, he got up and walked into her room. The chair was in the same place where he left it. Nothing was out of place in her room. With a shrug, he returned to the couch and attempted to immerse himself back in the game. That only lasted for several minutes before something else happened.

They had also relocated a large stand to his mother's room. It contained a fifteen-pound glass vase with a decorative towel on the front and a mirror on the back. Tony saw the vase fly out, nearly hit the eight foot ceiling before it bounced on the bed and crashed to the floor.

When Tony made it to the bedroom, he discovered that the towel that hung on the front was ripped off the stand and was also on the floor. In addition, the mirror that was mounted on the back of the stand was flipped backwards, so it was facing the wall. Tony couldn't believe what he saw.

He looked around for his nephews, but didn't see any sign of them. The room was empty and nothing else was amiss. With a pounding heart, he closed the doors and left the room, perplexed about what had just happened.

After the holiday festivities were over, Tony put the vase stand and Jim's rocking chair back in their normal places.

"I hope you're happy!" he said aloud to Jim. "Everything is back where you like it."

Later that night, he played video games in his bedroom, shutting off the television before going to sleep. He awoke at 3am to the sound of his bedroom door being opened. The room was pitch-black and he couldn't see a thing, but he could hear footsteps walking towards him. Not knowing who or what was causing the footsteps, he pulled the covers over his head and remained very still, mentally willing it to go away. After a minute, he heard the sound of heavy breathing, which was followed by the sound of footsteps moving back towards his door. The door closed and the room became silent once more.

As soon as the door closed, he sprang from bed and turned on the light. The room was empty. If someone had been there, there was no sign of it. Eventually, he calmed down enough to go back to sleep. The next morning, he went to turn on his TV and saw something that caused him to pause. In front of the "on button" was a stack of gold coins. There were exactly 33 of them.

He asked his mother about them, but she didn't know where they came from. In his heart, he knew it was Jim's way of thanking him for returning his chair to its rightful spot and apologizing for scaring him with his outburst of anger over the items being disturbed.

Chapter 9 - Music

When I'm traveling long distances, I like listening to my ITunes collection through my car stereo. I don't have to bother with songs I don't like and there aren't any commercials to contend with. During a recent trip, one deceased family member sent me a distinct warning.

Four songs with the word "angel" in the title played in a row. That definitely got my attention, since my music is set to play randomly.

I let them know I was listening and told them to give me the next sign, which was *The Kill (Bury Me)* by Thirty Seconds to Mars and then *Prayer* by Disturbed. With my heart hammering in my chest, I put on my blinker and got into the slow lane, reducing my speed down to 5 mph below the speed limit. Moments later, a pickup truck buzzed past quickly, weaving back and forth in the lane with obvious signs of driver inebriation. After that, the next song that came on was *Drive* by Incubus and then *Slow Ride* by Foghat. Message received, I drove a bit slower and made it home safely.

Needless to say, I frequently pay attention to the songs that come on my car radio. I wouldn't want to miss an important message.

***

Elizabeth Mourning-Bakker's story straddles two catagories. This story could easily be shared in the dreams section, but I thought the music aspect was fairly startling, considering the story.

After her brother Mitchell passed away in 2009, she's had many signs of him. This one is especially touching.

Elizabeth's Story

A couple years ago I woke up from the most strange, sad, and LOUD dream I remember having in a long, long time. There is a song by Lynyrd Skynyrd called *Simple Kind of Man.*

I had never in my life heard this song but somehow it was playing so loud in my dream that the walls and windows were rattling. It was so loud that it made my head hurt.

In the dream, my brother was at my house getting ready to leave. I do not know where he was going but he had to go somewhere. Someone was going to pick him up and I knew I would probably never see him again.

As we were gathering his things a car pulled up in the driveway and he said "There they are. I have to go." I walked him to the door and I hugged him and said "I will miss you."

He hugged me back and said "I will miss you too. I miss you so much (with an emphasis on the present.)"

He got in the car and left, and *Simple Kind of Man* was still playing as I watched the car back down the driveway. I had to Google the few words I remembered from the dream the next day to see if it was ever a real song. It still gives me the chills when I hear it.

***

Mary Lou Moriarty often comes to my Paranormal 101 classes and shared a story about her late father.

Her father had been gone for nearly a month when she woke up one morning with a song playing through her mind. The song was *Papa Can You Hear Me?* from the musical *Yentyl* with Barbara Streisand.

The song made her think of her father. He had always enjoyed singing and even sang in a choir. While she never heard him sing that particular song, it was bittersweet nonetheless. She's fairly certain he would have known it and would have appreciated her thoughts about him.

As she started her morning, she found herself singing the song aloud. Moments later, a spatula flew up out of a crock filled with utensils and landed on the floor beside her. It was one of the first signs he gave her.

The only problem was in determining if he liked the song or not. Mary-Lou said he had a great sense of humor, so he probably was playing a prank on her.

***

Charles Reis's mother Shirley Merton died in April of 2014. Charles was always close to his mother and the loss hit him hard.

His mother (*pictured left*) was a big fan of the band ABBA. After her passing, Charles started hearing

ABBA songs at odd times, making him wonder if she was attempting to communicate with him.

Shortly after her funeral, Charles signed onto YouTube. The first thing that showed in his subscriptions was "Top Ten ABBA Songs." The next time he signed on, he clicked on a link to a paranormal video and the suggested page beneath it was "The Best of ABBA."

A week later, he was walking down the street in West Warwick when something in the window of a consignment shop caught his eye. It was an ABBA album. The signs were piling up, one after another. It was more than he could brush off as coincidence.

Two months later, he had the opportunity to travel to Wales in the United Kingdom. While there, he went to Ogmore Castle and was planning on leaving his mother's prayer card in the castle ruins as a tribute to her, but forgot.

After touring the castle, he and a friend went to a small tea house nearby. After the waitress took their orders, she turned on the radio. The next song that came on was *Winner Takes it All* by ABBA. Knowing it was another sign from his mother, he returned to the castle after their meal and made sure to leave her prayer card in the ruins (see photo below).

Shortly after leaving the castle, someone snapped a picture of Charles. In it, you can see a streak of light that appears to come down from the heavens. Charles initially dismissed it as simply the light coming through the clouds, but after all the other signs he received, he gave it more relevance. After showing the photo to a psychic medium, she agreed with him. It was a sign from his mother. She was happy that he thought of her and left the prayer card in her memory.

(Above) Charles Reis in Wales and the sign of his mother

The signs of music continued. Charles still sees and hears references to his mother's favorite band.

"She was smart to use ABBA," Charles said. "While she was a fan of Reba in later years, if I would have heard a Reba song I would have paid no attention to it, but ABBA... yes," he said.

The music was especially appropriate. Not only was his mother a big fan of the group, it was the music he played for her the last night she was alive in hospice care.

Charles was told that she died with a smile on her face, something that helped ease the blow of her passing.

It makes sense to me that our loved ones would send us music signs after their passing. Music is often a tremendous part of our lives. When we hear certain songs, it often connects directly to a memory, bringing us a clear message.

***

For Jerry Lister, the music choice was especially appropriate.

On September 2nd, 2010, Jerry Lister was driving in his car, thinking about his father. It would have been his father's birthday, so his dad was on his mind.

He found himself talking to his father, wishing him a happy birthday. As he drove, he began surfing the radio stations, looking for some good music. The second station that came on startled him. It was playing *My Way* by Frank Sinatra. This was his father's favorite song.

He sang along, knowing that his father sent him that message and was probably singing along in Heaven.

Chapter 10 - Photos

*P*hotos should be one of the most recognizable signs of a deceased loved one, but the advance in technology has changed all that.

It's far too easy to digitally manipulate a photograph using phone apps and photo enhancing programs such as Photoshop or Gimp. Even if you capture something truly monumental, most people won't believe that it hasn't been altered. They've been duped too many times before to believe everything they see at face value.

Another problem with spirit photos has to do with the brain itself. As human beings, we are predisposed to search for faces in photos. It isn't difficult for us to find faces in trees, clouds and on reflections on windows and mirrors. The phenomenon is called pareidolia.

Within this frame of thought comes the ever popular orb photo. While it makes perfect sense that a spirit would take the most economical shape, which would be a round globe shape, it's far too easy to replicate such images. Dust and moisture in the air often reflects when hit with the light from a camera flash. It appears as a round glowing ball that seemingly hovers in the photo. People who have lost loved ones often reach for such images for signs they are receiving a message, but often it's just a case of a camera doing its job.

As a paranormal author and teacher, I'm often sent orb pictures. When I see them, I always think back to my very first ghost walk in Nashville, Tennessee.

The walking tour of Nashville was intriguing, showing us parts of the city we might not have seen otherwise, but the ghost walk was laughable. The guide brought us to the sidewalk across from the state house and waited for the stop light to turn red. As soon as the cars whizzing past came to a stop, he instructed us to take photos, using the flash on our cameras.

As can be expected, everyone had dozens, if not hundreds, of orbs in their photos. Many of those people walked away thinking they had captured a ghost, while in reality all they got was photos of road dust.

The only time I will take an orb photo seriously is when it is caught in motion on video, taking a path that isn't normal for dust or moisture. Even this is difficult to evaluate due to the unknown factors that occurred when the photo was taken. Were there heat vents anywhere near the photo that might cause the dust to move through the air? Was there a window open somewhere outside the frame of the photo that would cause an air disturbance? Unless I'm on sight when the photo or video is captured, I can't properly validate its authenticity.

***

Some signs are difficult to dismiss so quickly. One case is the story that Kerri Wilson Stringfield sent me.

After her young son passed away, Kerri was desperate for a sign from him. He was sick for a long time, spending weeks in a hospital fighting for his life. When he succumbed to his illness, his parents were appropriately devastated.

Like any mother would be, Kerri was anxious to know that he was okay.

At his funeral, they released several dozen yellow balloons. Joey always loved balloons and yellow was his favorite color. As the balloons floated away, they briefly formed the shape of a heart in the sky as a single bird flew past them. Kerri took it as a sign that Joey was finally at peace.

She also captured an interesting photo of her mother-in-law sitting in a chair. In the background, it appears that light is shining on a sofa. If you zoom in closely, it appears to be a face that looks remarkably like her son, Joey. Kerri finds it especially interesting because right before she took the photo, a medium friend called her and told her that she would be getting a sign soon. After she snapped the photo, she knew that her sign had finally come.

(Above: Left-zoomed in section of sofa. Right-photo of Joey)

***

Gina Bengtson is a paranormal investigator with an arsenal of equipment that most other investigators would drool over. As the co-host of a popular online radio show, *Second Sight Radio* with Chris George, she often takes on various paranormal topics, which makes her well-versed in the field.

I first met Gina at the 2015 Salem-Con, a paranormal themed convention where I rented a booth to peddle my paranormal books. Even though we'd been chatting on social media for some time, we had never met in person. It was an instant friendship, one of those rare occurrences that feels more like fate than circumstance.

Since that point in time we've become good friends and have shared several paranormal adventures as we've explored vacant buildings and haunted establishments.

By looking at her, you'd never know the heartbreak Gina has lived through. She's an upbeat person with an infectious smile and is always looking out for everyone else. The way she bounced back from such tragedy shows the depth of her character.

In 2003, she was happily married to the love of her life. Mark was an avid fisherman and hunter and enjoyed being outdoors. The two purchased a camper together and spent long weekends exploring New England together. Gina thought he was her forever love. That all ended abruptly in 2011, when she came home to discover that he had died of a sudden heart attack.

Losing him was devastating, but Gina somehow pulled herself through it. She knows that Mark is still around, helping her deal with the loss. She's felt him numerous times.

Being a paranormal sensitive, Gina can feel the presence of ghosts and spirits around her. Sometimes she can hears a tone, similar to the way that I detect ghosts. Other times, she just knows they are there. She then validates her impressions with her paranormal equipment.

After Mark died, she couldn't bear to keep the sofa that he died on, but she did hold onto the pillow his head had rested on. One night when she was feeling as though Mark was nearby, she snapped a photo of the pillow with her thermal camera. The image she saw looked exactly like Mark did when she found him after he died.

Even though she encourages him to move on, she knows that he's still nearby, watching over her. Although he can't be here in a physical form, the love he feels for her is eternal. It might not have been the "happily ever after" Gina was hoping for, but it is a love that will never die.

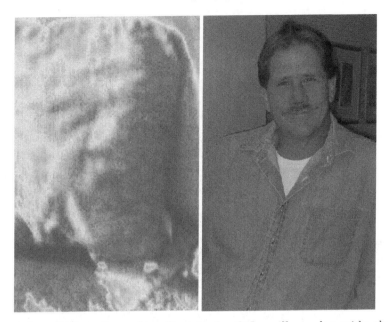

(Above) The photo that Gina took of the pillow alongside the picture of her late husband Mark.

Chapter 11 - Animals and Pets

Sometimes the signs of a deceased loved one might come with the arrival of an animal, insect or bird. Duckie DuBois found this out first-hand at her aunt's burial. As they stood outdoors, a butterfly landed on her mother's arm.

"A butterfly just landed on me," her mother said, stunned. Everyone watched with amazement as the butterfly took flight and went directly to one of Duckie's aunts and landed on her arm as well. It then flew to the next aunt and visited for a moment, not stopping until it had landed on every one of Duckie's aunts. Then it took flight and flew away, leaving them all with the memory.

If the loved one was someone who was also fond of your pets, your cat or dog might see them and react to them. Does your dog sometimes wag his tail while staring across the room? Does your cat start purring for no apparent reason? Both dogs and cats have far superior hearing than we do. They can pick up sounds that expand beyond the scope of normal human hearing. Their sight is also different, allowing them to see further into the red spectrum.

My adventurous cats often watch things float around my bedroom. At times, they watch with such focused attention, I would swear there was a bug moving around the room.

Paranormal investigators often bring dogs with them to investigations, watching their reactions to areas where paranormal activity is known to happen. I've investigated with several sensitive canines and have found their behavior to be intriguing. As someone who is also sensitive to the energy ghosts and spirits emit, I'm often pulled to the same areas that the dogs are drawn to.

Pets often come back to visit after they've passed too. Signs of their presence will be similar to the habits they followed in life. They will sleep in their favorite places and jump up on beds and couches with a pronounced landing. If your cat often liked knocking the knick-knacks off your mantel, you might find them on the floor on occasion after his passing, as well.

I've written about my friend Sandy and her ghosts cats in many of my books and articles. Her cats have been coming back for visits for years. One of the first cats to visit was Gremlin, who liked to sit on her shoulders, both in life and in death. When she felt his comfortable weight on her shoulder several years after he passed, she knew he came back for a visit.

Several more of her cats have come back to visit as well. She often feels them pounce on the bed, sometimes even witnessing the mattress depress from their invisible weight.

After the death of my own cat Gatorbug, I hoped to have a sign of my own, similar to Sandy's experience. I missed him so much.

I adopted Gatorbug from a shelter when he was just a kitten and formed a deep bond with him. Being an avid animal lover, he became as close to me as family. He slept with me every night and was never more than an arm's length away for most of the day.

When he developed diabetes, I had to give him insulin injections twice a day and put him on a structured diet. Gone was the never-ending supply of dried food and in its place came twice a day feedings of a diet he didn't care for.

(Above) The author with her beloved cat Gatorbug in 2011

Much to his credit, he adapted quickly though. He began finding me hours before his feeding and giving me "that look" that most cat owners are well familiar with as he politely asked for his next meal.

For the next two years, we struggled to regulate his blood sugar. Even with the special diet, he often fluctuated.

Eventually, it became too much for his body and he went into a series of seizures that he couldn't come out of, and I was forced to have him euthanized.

Ironically, I was on the phone with Barbara Williams when it happened. She connected with Gatorbug while we were on the phone and told me that he'd already checked out. "He might still be physically alive, but he left his body after the first seizure. He basically said, 'I'm out of here!' and was gone."

Her words helped me make the decision to put him down. The veterinarian had little other suggestions and felt that the damage was so severe, he'd never recover even if the seizures miraculously stopped.

Saying goodbye to him was one of the hardest things I've ever had to do. For some people, he was just a cat, but he was much more to me. He saw me through some rough times and was my comfort when I had nobody to talk to.

I hoped he would come back to visit like Sandy's cats did, but it took him nearly a year. One day, as I was leading my normal parade of cats to the kitchen for their evening feeding, I saw a dark shadow zip past.

I did a double-take because I could clearly see all my other cats far ahead of me. There was nothing that should have caused that small cat-sized shadow. It wasn't until I saw it several more times that I realized what it was. Gatorbug was back, enjoying his favorite part of the day.

***

I've had an affinity for African Clawed Frogs since my daughter was a child and someone gave her a froglet kit as a gift. We set up the environment and mailed off for the tadpole, which should have been delivered in the mail several weeks later. Being that it was the heart of winter, they didn't feel that a tadpole would survive the trip to the frigid northeast, so they sent us a baby frog instead.

We received the froglet weeks later and then received the promised tadpole as soon as the weather grew warmer. The two frogs seemed very fond of one another, which stood to reason since one was a female and the other was a male. Low and behold, the following year, the female laid hundreds of eggs inside their aquarium.

(Above) Matild, the author's African Clawed Frog

I saved many of the eggs and allowed them to hatch into froglets. At one point, I had thirty baby frogs in my aquarium.

I loved watching them. They became pets in a way, watching me when I came into the room. They would all swim to the surface, begging to be fed.

Unfortunately, while I was away for a few days, a malfunctioning filter caused a mass casualty. I came home to discover that all my frogs were dead, including the parents.

Several years later, I was in a pet store and saw an albino African Clawed Frog for sale. It was a tiny little thing, no bigger than the tip of my thumb.

"You know they can grow to be over ten inches long and can live to be twenty years old, right?" the clerk asked me. I smiled, remembering how large mama frog became, and happily took home my new pet.

I named her Matilda because it seemed like a proper frog name. Like her predecessors, she quickly grew from a thumb-sized froglet to a massive ten inch frog. I kept her in my kitchen in a ten gallon aquarium for nearly ten years.

She became a beloved pet, just like my other critters. I couldn't pick her up or hold her, but she showed her affection in other ways. She would take food right out of my fingers and would nuzzle my hand if I put it in the water. When she came down with bloat after being moved from one house to another, I tried in vain to cure her, but the damage was done. Stress, along with a change of water properties eventually did her in.

When I came into the kitchen and found her floating at the top of the tank, the grief was real. I cried as hard as I did when my cat died. Matilda was a pet and I grew attached to her.

I buried her outside and put a large stone on top of her grave to mark the place. That night, when I went to bed, I thought about her, wishing I would have taken more care in moving her. I should have brought more water from my first home to better acclimate her. I allowed the guilt to grow and flourish, leaving me restless. When I was finally able to fall asleep, I had a dream about her.

In the dream, I was wading through a stream. The water was warm and clear. It came up to my knees as I made my way through it. Without warning, I turned to see a tiny white frog swimming beside me. It looked exactly like Matilda did as a baby.

As I watched in stunned surprise, the froglet swam up beside me and touched my leg. I awoke with a smile on my face. People might tell me that it was just a dream, but I know in my heart that Matilda came back to tell me that she was young and healthy again.

Animals that come to us don't necessarily have to be pets though. People often feel that wild life, including birds, mammals and insects come as signs from loved ones.

When people tell me their stories, they almost always ask me if I think it was a sign. From my perspective, it's almost impossible to know for certain. I usually ask them what they thought when they saw it. If they thought about a loved one, then it probably came from them. They often give us the mental thought of them at the same time they send the sign, just to be sure we understand.

In many cultures, people believe that the type of animal makes a difference in the message too. Animal totems are signs from our spiritual allies, providing us with messages.

Several weeks ago, I was on the same long, boring highway I always traverse on my way to teach my Paranormal 101 classes. On this particular day, I was feeling immense stress. Being a self-published author can be quite demanding. Considering that I live in one of the most expensive areas of the country, it's often difficult to make ends meet. As I drove, I was attempting to figure out what I could do to bring in more money. At the same time, I found myself plummeting into the pit of despair. Was it always going to be this way? In order to do what I love, do I need to always struggle financially?

As those words flitted through my mind, a magnificent bald eagle swooped down from the sky. I wasn't even aware they were indigenous to my area of the country. The only time I've ever seen one was in a zoo.

I slowed down, marveling in the sheer beauty and grace of the bird. As if showing off, it tilted sideways with its wings spread wide, showing me its sleek outline and snow white tail feathers. Then, as though it was making sure I got the message, it landed on a low hanging tree branch just before I drove under, watching me with a careful eye. Interestingly enough, I was on my way to teach a class on Animal Spirit Guides.

Some people are aware that they have spirit guides to help them through their lives, but most people don't realize that they also have animal spirit guides. Some stick with us for the duration of our lives, while others pop in to deliver specific messages. As soon as I got to class, I jumped online to look up the meaning of a bald eagle.

I couldn't have been more astounded when I read it. It said that if you see a bald eagle animal totem, it means to listen to your intuition and soar above all your doubts to follow your dreams. Message received!

***

Lisa Robichaud St. Pierre also had an experience with an animal message. Her story shows the importance of listening to what is sent to you.

Lisa's Story

I lost my father on October 13, 2007. We were always very close and I was definitely "Daddy's Little Girl." My father was diagnosed with lung cancer in June of 2007, though he never smoked, he also had the beginning stages for idiopathic pulmonary fibrosis (which is eventually fatal). This was a difficult time for both of us.

I think the hardest thing for him was the role reversal. I was driving him into Boston for chemo and radiation. I was pushing him in a wheel chair when he was too weak. I badgered him to drink plenty of water, I became his maternal figure.

Treatment actually went better than they had expected. They actually eradicated the cancer, but the doctors wanted to do one more round of radiation as a prophylactic measure.

My father insisted that he couldn't handle it because he felt too poorly. If you knew him, you would realize that something was very wrong. He had a high tolerance for pain and he would go to work with the plague before calling in sick.

Come to find out, the radiation had exacerbated the pulmonary fibrosis and my father's lungs were struggling to do their job. He was then intubated and put on a respirator in hopes of giving his lungs a rest and possibly repair themselves to some extent.

They took him off the ventilator for a day and his symptoms became worse again. They had to put him back on the respirator. Once more they removed the breathing tube and this time, his breathing became very labored. At this point, the prognosis was bleak.

I didn't come from a demonstratively affectionate family. There was no hugging or crying. My dad asked me to replace my mother as his healthcare proxy. He knew that she would be unable to make a selfless decision, when and if the time came. My father made it very clear to me that he did not want to wake up on a respirator, with a feeding tube. He also added: make sure you do what is in accordance with the church (I grew up in a staunch Roman Catholic family).

They had to put him back on the respirator and after several hours the medical staff informed me that my father was no longer breathing on his own. After family was able to say their good byes, I asked the Dr. to take him of the ventilator. To be honest, I still do not know if that was in accordance with the church. I could not bear to see my father suffer.

I figured, it was my sin, not his, if it was not right with the Catholic Church. (I had been a "fallen Catholic" for years, per my father).

I held my father's hand as he passed with barely a gasp.

When my husband and I returned home at approximately 10:30pm, I was still on autopilot. I noticed the birdfeeders needed seed. I have my feeders hanging on the farmers porch, so I started to fill them and my husband followed suit.

Out of nowhere, a little gray bird (tufted titmouse I believe) started flying under the porch roof and swooping down us at least three or four times and then flew away.

It was nighttime and it was dark and I have never encountered such a thing. My husband and I looked at each other and we just knew! A few days later, I researched the symbolism of a bird after death. One article described a bird as a vessel which escorts a soul to heaven. I know that is true.

***

For others, the sign of an animal has more significant meanings. Suppose your mother always loved cardinals and one continued to land near your window after she died. This is something that happened to a woman named Jennifer.

After several loved ones passed away in a matter of a year, she found herself sinking into a deep depression. Not long after, a bright red cardinal began pecking at her window. He didn't just land on the windowsill, he seemed insistent that he wanted to come inside. She noticed it because it seemed to come when she was at her lowest.

As she recognized it as a possible sign, she felt herself coming out of the depression. Knowing that her passed-on loved ones were watching out for her was tremendously helpful.

***

Maria De Fatima also had an experience with cardinals. She had been close with her father, who had always loved cardinals. After he died, she began seeing a single red cardinal in a pear tree outside her house.

She walked outside with her camera and spoke to the bird.

"Dad, if that's you, then you will let me take a picture and you won't fly away," she said, calmly approaching the bird. The bird allowed her to get within touching distance without even fluttering a feather. He sat still until she took the picture and then flew off into the distance.

***

For Kristin, the sign was butterflies. Her mother's death hit her hard and was difficult for her to handle. When she got married several years later, thoughts of her mother accompanied her throughout the day. She wished her mother could have been there with her. It didn't seem fair.

After the wedding, they released a boxful of butterflies. Most of them flew straight up into the sky, happy for their freedom, but two of them stuck around. They kept landing on her and wouldn't leave. In her heart, she knew it was her mother and her grandmother, who had also passed away, letting her know that they did attend the wedding and were there to share in her joy.

According to psychic medium Barbara Williams, loved ones often send animals as signs, especially if the animal that is represented is something that was important to the loved one sending it.

One time, Barbara was doing a reading for a woman who had recently lost her mother. The woman's mother was always fond of hummingbirds. She kept multiple feeders outside her windows and even collected jewelry and decorative items with hummingbirds on them.

While Barbara was doing the reading, a hummingbird flew to the window beside them. Barbara thought this was odd since she didn't have any hummingbird feeders nearby. The bird hung there long enough for both women to see it before it took off again. It returned four more times during the reading, something neither Barbara nor the woman could miss. It was a sign that her mother is happy and in a good place, something the woman found comforting.

"Things that are out of the ordinary are things I look at," Barbara said. "Very often, the person themselves will intuit that that is a message from their loved one. We're so prone to second guessing ourselves, we often miss the message," Barbara added.

***

Patti Smith has been a friend for several years. I met her through a mutual friend at an investigation and have enjoyed getting to know her better on social media. Here's Patti's story.

Patti's Story

My mom who passed in June 2012 was my best friend. I told her everything and she always knew what to do or say. She was sick for a while with pulmonary hypertension which was secondary to scleroderma. She was on oxygen 24/7.

When my dad passed in November 2010, she got depressed, and I knew she wanted to be "home" with him. I took her to all her doctor's appointments, visited her every day and cooked her dinner every night before I went home.

(Above) Patti and her mother in 1996

She knew I was into the paranormal and she always told me when she passed she would give me a sign and boy did she.

The day she passed I will never forget.

She called me at 8:30 in the morning. At the time, I lived an hour and a half away, so I knew I wouldn't get to her fast enough. I called my ex-husband who passes her house to go to work and asked him to stop and check on her. He did and called me to tell me he was calling the ambulance and to meet at the hospital.

I couldn't get there fast enough. As I went in, I had my two girls with me and we rushed to her room in the ER. She was smiling and cracking jokes like she always does, so I figured everything would be okay.

The hospital did all their tests and took her up to ICU. They said they would get us from the waiting room when she was all set up. Luckily my brother was up from Georgia on vacation so we all sat waiting.

When no one came for over an hour, I decided to take my oldest daughter and go check. We walked to the room that was filled with doctors and nurses and my Mom was talking to them. One of the doctors came out to talk to me as my mom was signing the DNR (Do Not Resuscitate) paper. He proceeded to tell me my mom was terminal and it would only be a couple days at best.

At that moment, the nurse started calling my mom's name over and over. I told my oldest daughter to go get her uncle. I rushed into the room and held my mom's hand as my brother came in and held her other hand. At that moment, I told her it was okay, she could go see Dad again and she took her last breath.

A couple days later, we were all sitting in my living room when out of nowhere, a Luna Moth, which I have never seen before, flew into the room and landed right on my hand. It wouldn't leave.

I proceeded to take it outside and close the door. Again the moth found its way back into the living room, landing on my hand. I left it in the living room and the next morning it was gone.

The day after her funeral, I decided to put a voice recorder on the kitchen table as we were all sitting around talking about the good old days.

I blamed myself for my mom's passing, thinking there was more I could have done. That night, as I was listening to anything we could have caught, I heard my mom, plain as day, say, "Patti, it's not your fault."

I still have that recording and when I get down thinking I could have done more, I listen to it.

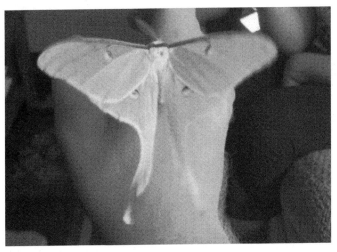

(Above) The Luna Moth that landed on Patti's hand

***

Amy Christensen is a nurse who works at a nursing home. Years ago, they had a cat named Molly who had full run of the facility. The residents loved Molly, since she brought them comfort. She was a calm cat who enjoyed being held and petted, which was a perfect situation for everyone.

Normally, Molly wasn't particular about which room she visited. She roamed the entire facility at will. Soon though, that all changed.

The staff began noticing that there was actually a pattern to Molly's visits. Molly would pick a room and spend several days with the patient. Within a week of her visit, the patient would die.

The staff began keeping an eye on Molly after that, astounded at her accuracy. It often gave them a better indicator on the patient's health situation, something they could use to the patient's advantage.

Molly was eventually relocated to a staff member's house, but no one will ever forget the comfort she gave those she loved.

***

I've known Twana McRae since I was a baby. Since our parents were friends, we would often play together while our parents socialized. Twana is serious and straight-forward and was perhaps one of the last people I expected to come to me with a story about a deceased loved one visiting. She actually shared two stories with me. Here is the first one.

Twana was always her grandmother's favorite out of all her grandchildren. She was with her grandmother when she died.

After her grandmother's funeral, going back to work the first day was difficult for Twana. As she came home that night, exhausted from a long day, she was amazed to see her dog Teddy standing at the end of her long driveway where it met with the road.

She never left Teddy loose. Usually he was either kept inside the house or was inside the fenced-in yard. She grabbed him and drove up the driveway, thankful he hadn't gotten hit by a passing car.

When she walked inside with Teddy, she was astounded to find her outside dog inside the house. The larger dog was never allowed in the house. Twana raced upstairs to talk to her kids, who had no idea what had happened. Neither of them let Teddy out or the other dog in.

Later, she found a framed photo of her grandparents knocked off a high shelf with the glass cracked. Instinctively, she knew it was her grandmother, leaving her a sign. Her grandmother had never been an animal lover, but she knew she wouldn't do anything to hurt her. Perhaps, she just wanted to get Twana's attention in the way she knew would have the greatest impact.

*****

Before they moved to their old farm house, Chontel MacMunn and her husband inherited a beautiful long-haired cat. She had been left behind at the place they previously rented and was very shy at first.

Chontel felt bad for the cat, who she began calling Mikki. She'd lived at the house with people who cared for her only to have them suddenly leave without taking her with them. Chontel kept thinking the people were going to come back to get her, so she didn't want to get too attached, but she couldn't help it.

Mikki was a beautiful cat. She had a long bushy coat, making Chontel wonder if she was part Maine Coon. When she ran, she held her tail straight up like a flag. She also had a sweet personality, despite being skittish and afraid.

Chontel was patient with her, knowing the cat had endured great hardship in her young life. After several weeks of quietly coaxing her, she finally began to trust them. Mikki began coming indoors to be fed and would brush their fingers when they reached out to her.

(Above) Chontel MacMunn's cat Mikki

What made Chontel believe that Mikki really belonged with them came after Chontel developed a foot injury, which took her off her feet for an extended period of time. Since she couldn't climb the stairs, she began sleeping on the couch. One night as she reclined on the couch, Mikki climbed up beside her. Chontel began petting her and she responded by putting her paw on Chontel's hand, as though holding it in place. The cat hardly left her side the entire time she was incapacitated.

Five years after they found Mikki, another cat came into their lives. Kramer was just a kitten when he moved in with them. At first, the two cats were wary of one another, but that faded over the course of a few weeks. They became fast friends.

When Chontel and her husband moved to the farmhouse, Mikki and Kramer settled in, becoming true members of the family. The two cats developed a close bond and were seldom out of one another's sight.

During the summer months, Chontel didn't keep a litter box in the house. Instead, she let the cats go outside to do their business. They seemed to enjoy being outdoors to hunt bugs and play in the grass, so it seemed like a beneficial arrangement.

One day, while Chontel and her husband were in New York City visiting with their oldest son, her youngest son was home with the pets. When Mikki scratched at his door wanting to be let out, he happily complied. When he went outside later, he discovered that Mikki had been hit and killed by a passing car.

The family was distraught by the loss of their beloved pet. By the time Chontel got home, Mikki had already been buried in the backyard.

She put flowers on her grave and talked to her. In the meantime, Kramer was distraught. He seemed to search the house, looking for her, crying incessantly.

Chontel felt bad for all of them. Losing a pet was like losing a member of the family. She had a deep attachment to all her pets. It was something you just didn't get over. Their loss left a hole in her life, one she could never fill again.

Not long after Mikki died, they began seeing something strange inside the house. As Chontel sat on the couch, watching television, she saw the flash of Mikki's bushy tail as she raced up the stairs.

Was that really Mikki? Did she come back?

Once she and her husband realized what they were seeing, they began seeing it more and more. They'd catch flashes of her and see her bushy tail held high like she always held it. She would often race silently up the stairs. The only thing missing was the pitter patter of her paws as she climbed the steps. They saw her for a month or two and then it stopped altogether.

(Above) Kramer with Sadie

After nearly two years following the sightings, they began hearing a strange tapping sound in the northwest corner of their living room. It happened during the day and the night. If one of them went to look, the sound would disappear as quickly as it started. Not long after the tapping sounds started, Kramer began to act strangely.

They brought him to the vet and learned that he had diabetes, but it was too late to treat him. He was already twelve years-old by that time and the doctor didn't feel the treatments would be helpful. Instead, Chontel and her husband brought him home to keep him comfortable so he could live out his remaining days.

Chontel began to wonder if Mikki came back to escort her brother across the rainbow bridge. Once Kramer passed, they never saw Mikki again, so she believes that to be true.

A few years later, her younger son adopted a dog he named DeNiro (*pictured on the left*). DeNiro was a black and white pit bull/bulldog mix with a cheerful, loving personality. He'd put his head on the arm of the chair as he'd lovingly watch them walk by. When he wanted to play, he'd get down on the ground and move his paws like he was marching. He was a true charmer.

As a puppy, he had far more energy than their older dogs could handle at times. When he got overly rambunctious, they would put him in the kitchen behind a baby gate to give their older, more delicate, dogs a break. In many ways, he was like a toddler in a nursing home.

One day, Chontel's husband took him outside to go to the bathroom. Once DeNiro was finished, he brought him back into the kitchen so he could let the older dogs out.

While her husband was outside with the other dogs, DeNiro somehow managed to get the kitchen door open and bolted outside, wanting to play. His momentum was so fast, he couldn't stop. He ran into the road and was immediately hit and killed by a passing car. It was another devastating loss.

A month later, Chontel and her son were sitting in the living room when they heard a familiar bark coming from the kitchen.

She sat up on the couch, shocked at what she heard. It was DeNiro. His bark was distinctive. She'd know it anywhere.

She called out to her husband. "Did you hear that?"

"Hear what?" he said.

"DeNiro, barking from the kitchen."

Her husband came into the living room with a perplexed look on his face. Even though he was in the room where the sound originated, he didn't hear a thing.

Not long after that, they began hearing the tapping sounds again in the northwest corner of the living room. After living through it with Kramer, they had a pretty good idea what it meant.

Their older dog Sadie had just been diagnosed with cancer and there wasn't much they could do for her. Chemo would have only given her another additional month to live and they didn't want to put her through that.

It crushed Chontel to see her Sadie so sick. Sadie was a black lab/golden retriever mix. She had a silky black coat and a sweet disposition.

When it got to the point where Sadie was suffering, they knew it was time to call the vet. She couldn't get up any more and had stopped eating for several days.

The vet came to their house to euthanize her. They wanted Sadie to be comfortable in their home, surrounded by the people she loved when she passed.

As the veterinarian put the needle into her arm, Sadie turned her head and looked at Chontel's husband. Then, just like that, she was gone. It had only been a month since DeNiro died.

(Above) Penny and Sadie

The next day, Chantel was walking into the kitchen when something caught her attention. From the corner of her eye, she saw Sadie standing outside at the corner of the walkway facing the house. When she turned with a gasp to look, the dog vanished.

It happened again the next day, as well. This time was different though. As she looked for Sadie, she didn't just fade away. She was just gone. Chontel took it as a sign that Sadie was leaving them, that she had come back one last time to say goodbye.

The following year, little Penny grew ill with pancreatitis. They had her on medication but she wasn't responding to treatment. When they began hearing the tapping from the northwest corner of the living room, they knew her time with them was growing shorter. Several days later, she died in their bed as she lay between Chontel and her husband.

Chontel and her husband haven't had another animal companion since then. Loving them came so easy, but losing them had been harder than she could handle. They're all buried in her yard, the place they loved the most. Chontel visits their graves frequently to let them know she will never forget them.

***

Pets often come back in various fashions. Some will appear visually, while others show us with other signs. For Cheryl Phillips, it was an unmistakable sound.

Their dog Sunshine was hit and killed by a car when she chased after a jogger. The family was crushed by the loss.

Several days after her dog's death, Cheryl heard the unmistakable sound of Sunshine scratching at their door, like she always did when she wanted to come inside.

Cheryl opened the door, not seeing anything, but she knew who was there.

"Come on in, Sunshine," she said. "We've missed you."

She never heard the sound again.

(Above) Cheryl's dog Sunshine

***

For Tammi Campbell Quick, the signs were unmistakable. The night after their cat Pixie died, she came back to say goodbye.

She was sleeping when she heard the sound of her bedroom door creaking open. It was followed by the meow of a cat as it greeted her.

They didn't have any other cats, so this was startling for her. She turned to look toward the doorway, but couldn't see anything in the darkness.

As she looked around the room, she felt a cat jump onto the bed and walk towards her. She held out her hand to touch it, but nothing was there.

(Above) Tammi Campbell Quick's cat Pixie

"Pixie?" she asked, turning on the nightstand light.

The room was empty. There weren't any cats in her room and there was no explanation for what had happened.

The next morning, she told her mother about her encounter and was surprised that her mother had nearly the same experience.

Pixie came back to say goodbye.

In some cases, the visitation is so real, people often mistake it for a live animal. After experiencing Pixie's reappearance, her mother told her about something else that had happened to her years ago.

Their neighbor had a beagle named Becky they often kept in the garage. While they were gone, Becky bayed nearly all day long. After an especially grueling day of listening to the dog, they were happy when the neighbors came home because the barking stopped.

They walked over to tell the neighbors about Becky's obvious discomfort and were astounded to learn that the dog had died several days earlier.

The sound they heard came from beyond the grave.

Chapter 12 - Moved Items

When you place your reading glasses on your nightstand and find them on the kitchen counter, you might wonder if you've lost your mind.

I had this happen to me repeatedly until a psychic medium friend clued me in to what was really happening. A family friend, who often visited me in spirit form, liked to play pranks on me. She was simply trying to get my attention, doing something she might have done while she was alive. It made me feel much better knowing it was Betty and not the first signs of dementia.

Others might find more obvious signs, like a photo of the departed loved one that refuses to remain upright or a piece of jewelry that continues to turn up in odd places. This is especially significant if the jewelry or item once belonged to the person who is visiting you.

Barbara Williams calls this mysterious phenomenon "apporting." An apport is when an item disappears from location and reappears in another location.

"Sometimes, it's not so funny, especially if it's your keys and you need to get out of the house. If that happens, you need to have a conversation with them. Tell them to do it with something else and not when you're in a hurry," she said.

But, there could also be a message in the apporting. The spirits might be prompting us to slow down and not get caught up in the hurried pace of life.

***

A woman named Cindy commented on my Ghost Diaries article with an interesting story of her own.

She was quite ill a few years ago, to the point where her mother thought she would be burying her. During this time while she was in the hospital, she woke up to discover her father sitting on the end of her bed with her son on his lap.

This was surprising to her because her father died when she was in her twenties and her son is now the age she was when her father died. She took it as a sign that her father was still watching over her, but that it wasn't her time to go. She had too much to live for still.

While she was in the hospital, her necklace disappeared. She was crushed because she never took the necklace off. A few months after she was home from the hospital, she heard a loud crash coming from her bedroom. She was astounded to discover that her dresser had tipped forward, breaking a twenty-year-old bottle of whiskey that her father once owned. She cleaned up the mess and put the dresser back in place, feeling disheartened at the loss. When she came back into the kitchen, she stopped dead in her tracks. Her missing necklace was on the floor in front of the sink. She knew in her heart that her father had retrieved it for her.

I attempted to contact Cindy to learn more information, but never heard from her. I thought it was curious that the necklace disappeared and then reappeared after his bottle of whiskey was broken. Had someone at the hospital taken the necklace and her father returned it? Or had her father taken it for safe keeping? Either way, it's an intriguing story.

***

Another story came to me from a woman I met briefly at the Haunted Victorian Mansion, where I spent several years prior to writing my book about the previous owner's experiences there.

Melissa DiPetri was twenty years old when her grandmother passed away. The family was very close and were distraught at the loss, even though they knew it was inevitable. Melissa's grandmother had lung cancer, something she suffered with for three years before she passed away.

When her grandmother died, the family gathered at her parent's house. Wracked with grief over her passing, they were huddled together on her parent's bed, crying when something happened that jolted them away from their tears. The door to the bedroom flew open with a bang.

They sat up and stared at the door, shocked beyond belief.

"Was that the cat?" someone asked, trying to find a logical explanation for it.

They searched the house, only to find the cat curled up asleep on the couch downstairs.

Melissa will never know for sure what caused the door to open, but in her heart she believes it was her grandmother saying goodbye. "Because honestly after the door swept open, I felt a feeling of peace. It was lovely," she said.

After reading Melissa's story, the investigator in me started to raise her head, looking for ways to debunk the activity. After all, it could have been due to any number of circumstances. The wind could have shifted outside, causing pressure indoors that pulled the door open or it could have just been a door that was unevenly hung. What caused me to put aside my skepticism was the peace she felt when it happened. That is usually a very prominent sign of a passed on loved one.

***

For others, the signs are more perplexing.

When Jerry Lister's father passed away six years ago, he had just moved into a new house. His father died about four months after he moved into the house. The two of them were very close and he felt the loss like a hole in his soul.

Since his father's death, Jerry has asked his father for a sign of his presence. He feels as though his father is near, but he hadn't received any confirmation besides the song that played on the radio that I told in a previous chapter. He was hoping for something more, something more definite.

When strange occurrences started happening in his new home, he had to wonder if his father was behind it.

"For the last few years, a consistent sign that I receive is that the ceiling fan in my family room will automatically start spinning when clearly no one in the house has turned it on. It has occurred on about twenty occasions during the last two years," he told me.

"I was concerned enough that I had an electrician come and look at the connections to assure me that the wires were properly connected. He verified that they were. There have been times where I may have dreamed about my Dad and when I come from my bedroom into the family room, I'll find the ceiling fan spinning. On one occasion, I jokingly said, 'Ok, Dad, you can turn the fan off now,' and it stopped," he said.

Another odd synchronicity deals with the timing of the ceiling fan incidents. "My Dad and I shared a passion for sports. It bonded us. I have discovered that on the approximate 15 of the 20 or so occasions when this phenomenon happened I was watching a sporting event on TV. How would you explain this?" he asks.

I wouldn't even try to explain something like that. I would take it as a sign and say thank you.

***

Gina Bengtson shared another story with me about her late husband Mark, who passed away of a sudden heart attack in 2011.

One day, as Gina was tidying up the house, she saw Mark's wedding ring sitting on the dresser. She slipped it on her thumb, feeling a measure of comfort in having it nearby.

She wore it most of the day, not realizing it was missing until she was cleaning up her workshop. She had just returned from a painting job and had removed all the tarp and paint cans from her truck.

One of her tarps was covered in painter's tape and she had spent nearly fifteen minutes attempting to remove it. Once she pulled it off the tarp, she wadded it up and threw it into a basket on the floor. She was halfway through her clean-up when she realized the ring was missing.

"I pulled every tool bag apart and went outside, thinking I might have dropped it in the snow," she said. "I wracked my brain, trying to remember the last time I saw it, but I couldn't figure out where it went."

(Above) Gina Bengtson and her late husband Mark

Finally, after hours of searching for it, she decided to utilize her paranormal investigation equipment. She pulled out a digital recorder and turned it on.

"Mark, if you're there, please tell me where I lost the ring," she said.

As a paranormal investigator, she knew that voices from the dead aren't usually heard by the living. They often speak in a frequency that can't be detected by human hearing, but can be recorded digitally. When played back, a ghostly voice can be heard if they responded to the question.

This was the case for Gina. Very distinctly, she could hear a man's voice that sounded remarkably like Mark. It said. "It's in the bin."

She turned around and looked at the rows and rows of bins in her workshop. There were hundreds of them, all lined up on shelves to keep her tools and equipment neatly separated.

She started going through all the bins, but couldn't find it. She was ready to give up when she saw the basket on the floor.

Technically, it could be considered a bin, but it wasn't what she thought of when she thought of her bins. With a shrug, she bent down and began going through all the wads of painter's tape. As she was halfway through the basket, she stopped with a gasp. Stuck to a wad of tape was her husband's wedding band.

Mark had helped her find it, but as it turns out, it wouldn't be the last time he would help her. He might have even saved her life.

Gina had been cutting wood in her workshop for several hours one winter day. Since it was brutally cold outside, she turned on the space heater to stay warm, not thinking anything about it. She often used the space heater in the workshop and had never had any issues.

After she finished cutting the wood, she went upstairs to get a drink of water, thinking she'd come back later to turn the heater off. She sat down in her chair and inadvertently fell asleep.

The next thing she knew, she was torn from sleep by the sound of knocking and pounding coming from the basement. The sound was so loud, it almost sounded like someone was banging on pots and pans. She went downstairs to see what was going on.

When she opened the door to the workshop, the heat rolled out at her like air from a furnace. She could see the sawdust hanging in the air, seconds away from combustion.

"Oh my God!" she said as she raced to the garage doors. She opened the doors to air out the room and shut off the heater, never doubting that Mark had saved her from disaster. He might have even saved her life.

It's nice to know that our loved ones are looking out for us. While they can't interfere with our free will, if we ask them to always be there to help us, they will be.

***

For Crystal Pina, the message she got was both timely and thought provoking.

Ever since she's been an adult, her brother Derek has always called her at midnight on New Year's Eve. When he passed away quite suddenly in January of 2012, Crystal thought her annual New Year's well wishes were gone forever, but she got an amazing surprise.

The following New Year's Eve, she was sitting in bed, watching TV in her room with her husband. They had an empty gallon of water sitting on a nearby table. When the clock struck midnight, the cap on the jug flew up high into the air. Just before it hit the ceiling, it took a right angled turn in mid-air and flew across the room.

She and her husband looked at each other in shock. There was no way the water cap could have done that naturally. She knew in her heart that it was her brother's New Year's Eve message.

Later, she went to see a medium who confirmed that her suspicions were correct. Her brother did move the cap. She told Crystal that he's learning how to move objects and to expect more events in the future.

***

Like other signs, people often dismiss them as not being paranormal in nature. If a pair of eyeglasses is moved, people often make the logical assumption that they simply forgot where they placed them. Other times, it's far more difficult to explain. This was true in George Brun's case.

George Brun is a soft-spoken man who lives in New Hampshire. We met at a paranormal investigation and remained in contact over the years. George seems to have a knack for spirit photography and shared many of his amazing captures with me for my book *Ghostly Defenses*. When I asked for stories for this book, he was quick to email me with one.

In 1996, George's mother was put into a nursing home. Within a few months, she was sent to the hospital with chest issues. They gave her medication intravenously to alleviate the situation and she seemed to be responding well to the treatment.

At the time, George was recovering from spinal surgery and was confined to his bed. As he lay in his bed sleeping, a loud noise woke him. He looked up in time to watch his heavy television fall off the stand. Before he could truly react to it, the phone rang with a phone calling, informing him that his mother had just passed away.

In George's heart, he knows that it was his mother, making her presence known one last time.

***

Sometimes the items are more of a personal nature.

Cheryl Phillips also had an experience that she shared with me.

Her mother always used her father's cane after he passed away. She was meticulous about always putting it back in the same place when she wasn't using it and was surprised when it wasn't where it was supposed to be.

She searched the entire house looking for it. They couldn't find it anywhere. It was as though it simply vanished into thin air.

By the time three months passed without finding it, she thought it was gone forever. Imagine her shock when she came into the kitchen and found it hanging on the back of one of the kitchen chairs.

She never found out where the cane went and how it happened to end up back in the kitchen, but she was happy to have it back again.

***

When Bernice Perry's grandmother passed away, they weren't on the best of terms. As a remembrance of her grandmother, her mother gave her the Betty Boop doll that her grandmother had cherished.

Over the course of the next few months, Bernice began having dreams of her grandmother. In the dreams, her grandmother told her that she was sorry for the way things ended with the two of them. When she would wake up, the doll would mysteriously be moved from the shelf where she always kept it to an end table across the room.

Not only did her grandmother come to her in dreams, but she made sure Bernice knew about her visit by moving the doll.

In many of these stories, it strikes me as amazing how the personalities of our loved ones don't alter with death. If they were angry in life, they will be angry in death. If they were jovial in life, that too stays with them in death.

(Above) Betty Mayhan-Vlach and her Betty Boop doll

***

Elizabeth Mourning-Bakker shared several stories about her brother Mitchell, who passed away August 17, 2009. He has come to her, both in actions, words and dreams, showing that the soul is truly eternal and that love lives on. It also shows that a sense of humor also doesn't leave once we take our last breath.

Elizabeth's Story

Two years ago at Christmastime, my daughter and I were decorating our Christmas tree and putting up various Christmassy-type things. While hanging garland I accidentally knocked over a framed picture of my brother and daughter together, and it fell, breaking the glass.

As I turned to look down at the floor at the glass (my daughter was in the other room, thankfully), a Christmas ornament came flying at me sideways OFF OF THE TREE, and hit me in the face. I was nowhere near the tree and there is no way I could have knocked a Christmas ornament off of the tree to cause it to fly at my face in a horizontal fashion.

In my head I heard my brother's gruff laugh loud and clear. My immediate reaction was to say aloud "stop that!" I took it as him saying "that's what you get."

(Above) The photo of Elizabeth's brother Michael with her daughter that flew off the tree. You can see the cracked glass in the top left corner.

Pranks seem to be an amusing past-time on the other side. Whether it's ornaments flying off the tree, or in the following story, a door that shouldn't have been opened, our loved ones never stop trying to amuse us.

***

Sandra Chase has a linen closet just outside her bathroom. When the linen closet door is opened while someone is in the bathroom with the door closed, it essentially locks them in.

When her son was younger, he used to enjoy playing a joke on his father by opening the linen closet and then giggling as his father attempted to get out.

After her husband passed away on October 15, 2007, she thought the linen closet door pranks were a thing of the past, but that wasn't to be the case.

Thanksgiving day, she was at her nephew's house, while her now grown son was home alone at her house. When he went into the bathroom, he wasn't thinking about the pranks he pulled on his father, but when he tried to get out, he found himself stuck inside. Someone had opened the linen closet door while he was inside. Considering nobody else was at home, he knew exactly who to blame.

He and his mother shared a laugh over it later when she returned home and let him out.

Chapter 13 - Children Seeing Spirits

When I think about children seeing spirits, I remember the dream I had about my own grandmother shortly after she passed away. Children are often more receptive and open to communication than adults are. Some people say it's because they are closer to the time when they came into the world and haven't yet developed the filters that keep them from seeing the other side. Others believe that children are simply more intuitive.

If you have a child who seems to be communicating with someone you can't see, you should carefully and calmly assess the situation. Ask your child who he or she is talking to. If your child tells you it's a family member or someone you know who has passed on, try to get more details. Tell your child to ask validating questions that only the loved one could possibly answer correctly. Ghosts and other entities might attempt to masquerade as a loved on to gain your child's trust.

During this process, also get a sense of how the child is accepting this communication. Does it make her fearful? Or is your child nonplussed by the situation?

If you feel that the communication isn't healthy for your child, there are several steps you can take to alleviate the circumstances. Firstly, tell your child to stop all communication with it. Have her tell the "imaginary friend" that it is no longer welcome in the house and that it must leave. You can follow up with a house cleansing by burning a mixture of sage and sweet grass, filling your space with positive energy and removing any negative energy. More information about cleansing a house of ghostly energy can be found in my book *Ghostly Defenses*.

Children who frequently interact with the afterlife typically outgrow this ability by the time they are six or seven years old. If the ability continues after this age, you very might well have a budding medium in residence. Help them learn to harness and control their gifts while they're young, something that will help them contend with it when they're older.

If you discover that your youngster is indeed communicating with a deceased loved one, there is far less to worry about. More than likely, this spirit is looking after your child and will do anything to help keep him protected. Just monitor the situation as time progresses and keep tabs on the communication to insure it's both healthy and positive in nature.

For Wendy Brock Fox, the communication was nothing but positive, leaving her smiling with the memory.

Wendy's Story

My grandma always talked to my son about Jesus and how one day we could all walk the "golden streets" of Heaven to be with God.

My son was only two when she passed away. I had noticed several times where he was clearly interacting and laughing at something I couldn't see with my own eyes.

He had miniature angel chimes in his bedroom. I went to get him up from a nap and stopped when I heard him laughing and babbling like someone was in the room with him. I asked him who he was talking to and he told me it was G.G. - that's what he called her.

I was excited for him and told him, "Maybe the next time you can tell her I love her." At that very moment those little chimes started swinging slowly back and forth.

My son said, "You tell her, she's right there."

This is what blew my mind: Remember: he was only two years old when she talked to him about the "golden streets" of Heaven. He then told me, "She showed me heaven and she made it all the way to those "yellow roads"." Ughhh, still makes me cry.

In a follow-up, Wendy told me that her son is now 13 and still remembers his grandmother very clearly. He says he still misses her and remembers how she said he was her baby. She said she would always be with him, even when she goes to Heaven and would still visit him. She definitely fulfilled her promise.

***

Duckie DuBois also had an experience that left her puzzled.

Shortly after her step-father died, her granddaughter, who was twelve at the time called. She said, "Gram, did Grampa just die?"

Duckie wasn't sure what to say because she didn't know if her son had told her granddaughter the news yet. Instead of answering her, she asked her to explain why she asked.

Her granddaughter said, "Because he was just here and said goodbye to me and Maddy (her sister)." She said they didn't see him with their eyes, but could feel his presence. Both girls immediately began sobbing at the news, even though no one had officially told them. They knew it to be true.

***

When Amy Christenson was a child, she would have frequent conversations with who she thought was God. She often went into the woods and spent time in nature because she felt closer to God there. She also had invisible friends that she called "ghosties'.

When she saw them, they looked like cowboys on horses, except they were small like her. They reminded her of the images she saw in old movies about the Wild West. They were never threatening and she felt no fear when they were around. They seemed happy to know that she could see her and they spend long afternoons together, playing in the yard.

Years later, Amy learned that the land she grew up on was once the site of a Civil War battle. It made her wonder if the ghosties from her youth were actual people from the past, coming back to share some of their history with her.

***

These stories illustrate the amazing abilities most of us have while we're younger. Imagine if we didn't shut down that part of ourselves and allowed it to grow and flourish instead.

Fear is a powerful motivator. Most people who have encounters as children don't have the support and resources they need to handle it. This isn't something they often teach parents in parenting books.

Parents like Shawn and Mary-Jane O'Dou had to learn from scratch when both of their children exhibited mediumistic abilities from an early age.

When her daughter Shaely was only four, she began seeing scary visions in their Lake Pleasant, Massachusetts home. A creature she called "the monkey man" taunted her in the bathroom mirror as she brushed her teeth and a woman with broken legs often crawled across the living room floor.

Mary-Jane is no stranger to the paranormal world, having experienced several strange occurrences of her own as a child, so she knew what to do. She talked to her daughter and taught her how to protect herself by building a bubble of energy around herself, a process commonly called "shielding" in the paranormal community. She continued to monitor her daughter's experiences, calling in my group from time to time to cleanse the energy in her house and remove the entities.

What Mary-Jane didn't realize at the time was that her house was built on land that once served as a spiritual community. During the Spiritual Movement during the early part of the 1900's the land frequently saw thousands of visitors, hoping to communicate with the spiritual world. The land must have absorbed some of that energy, as well as retained some of the ghosts.

After her son Logan was born, he too began seeing things that no one else could see. When he was just a baby, he would fixate and smile at the air, as though he was seeing someone floating there.

Several months ago, Logan woke up from a nap and asked his mother where her father was. At three years-old, Logan was articulate and bright. It didn't surprise her that he would ask something like that. She explained to him that her father wasn't here anymore.

"Yes, he is," he said adamantly.

"No, honey. My father passed away before your sister Shaely was born," Mary-Jane explained to him.

Logan was growing agitated. "Yes, he is. He's in the living room by my trampoline."

Mary-Jane was used to Logan's unusual insights. Not long before that, he woke up to ask Mary-Jane to call his father to warn him about the rats. When Mary-Jane spoke with Shawn, he told her that when he got to work and opened a shed door, a large rat jumped out at him.

She didn't think that Logan had ever seen a picture of her dad, so she began quizzing him.

"What color hair did he have?" she asked.

"None, Mama. He's bald!" he said.

"What color were his eyes?" she asked.

"Blue!" She was astounded because that was a good description of her father. She pulled out a photo of her father later and showed it to Logan without telling him anything. He got excited.

"That's your dad!" he told her.

Just last week, Mary-Jane was curious if her dad was still around, so she asked Logan.

He shook his head. "No, he's at his house now."

"Where is his house?" she asked.

"It's way far away," he told her.

While it made Mary-Jane sad that her father was no longer around, she was glad to know that he got to see both of her children and communicate with them. Even though Logan never met him, it was obvious that they were still able to share a special bond.

Chapter 14 - Personal Contact

Making personal contact with loved ones is often very difficult for people who now reside in the spirit world. Learning how to "show themselves" to others is a skill that often takes years for them to master, but it's often the sign that most people yearn for the most.

In many ways, it is similar to the abilities that people learn while they're still alive. In my Paranormal 101 class, many of my students came to class for the first time with limited abilities. By working with the more gifted students in the class, they were able to expand on what they already knew.

A good example of this is Barbara Kirk Niles. We met at one of my book signings. As soon as she learned that I was planning to start teaching classes, she was one of the first to sign up.

When she first started coming to classes, she didn't feel that she had any abilities, but was willing to give it a try. Over the course of a year, she has uncovered talents she didn't know she had. She can feel when a ghost is nearby and can often get a mental image of what the soul looks like. She's currently working on learning how to shield herself from their energy, as well as knowing how to cross them over into the light.

145

She often feels her father around her and is working towards learning how to better communicate with him as well.

Imagine someone going into the spirit world with an inkling of this knowledge. Someone who is metaphysically gifted on this side of the veil might have a better idea of what is involved, but they would truly need to learn it from a different angle considering they no longer have a body. This might take them years, depending on their propensity for learning.

If a loved one comes to you in physical form, know that it is one of the biggest gifts they could give to you. The energy and intent it took them to show themselves was immense. They might only be able to hold the image for a moment before they disappear, while others seem to adapt quickly, remaining in clear focus for longer periods.

I'm especially happy when people I personally know share stories with me. I've known Marion Luoma for several years now and spent many hours in the very haunted S.K. Pierce Haunted Victorian Mansion where she is the caretaker. Before she became involved with the Victorian, Marion wasn't even remotely interested in the paranormal world. In fact, her first experience initially left her in denial.

In August of 1982, Marion and several family members drove back from Iowa from her sister Stacy's wedding. It had been a long drive and they were looking forward to finally getting home.

As they neared Highway 202, her mother who was in the car with her began having massive chest pains. As she pressed her hand to her chest, she said something strange.

"Something is wrong with the family," she said.

The chest pains immediately eased up, so they continued on their way home. As they came through the door, the phone was ringing. It was her mother's sister calling to tell them that Marion's grandfather had died. He died of an aneurism in his heart at the exact moment when her mother began having the strange chest pains.

It was difficult to sleep that night. She was close to her grandfather. When she first moved back to Massachusetts as a teenager, she lived with her grandfather for several years. When he needed something, they jumped in the car and headed to the store and often did yard work together too. Besides being her grandfather, he was also her Godfather. His death hit her hard.

After several hours of crying, she finally fell into a deep sleep. Halfway through the night, she was woken by the feeling of a hand caress her face. She opened her eyes and lay there for a moment, feeling the hand stroke her cheek before it trailed down to squeeze her shoulder.

She turned with a start to find her grandfather standing at the foot of her bed. Her breath caught in her throat as she stared at him. He had the same high hairline and mustache as usual. He wore dress pants and a long-sleeved dress shirt. The only thing that kept him from looking completely like he normally did was the fact that he was shaded like an old sepia photograph. As he moved, she realized she could see right through him. He gave her one last long look and then walked to the door and left.

Even though she knew it was him, she had a difficult time believing what she saw. The next morning, she searched the house for signs that someone had broken in during the night, but found nothing to corroborate the theory.

When she told her mother what she saw, a tear came into her mother's eye.

"You saw Grandpa. He came back to say goodbye to you," she said. It's a memory Marion will keep in her heart forever.

***

Elizabeth Mourning-Baker shared several stories about her experiences with her brother Mitchell, but none are more touching than the one below.

Elizabeth's Story

My brother, Mitchell, who I was very close to, passed away on Monday, August 17, 2009 at the age of fifty due to a massive heart attack. I have several stories to share about times I think he was trying to communicate with me from 'beyond'.

In the weeks and months after he passed away, I used to see what looked like camera flashes out of the corner of my eye. I saw them daily, dozens of times. I thought maybe my eyes were going due to long days behind a computer screen, but they eventually slowed to just a few a day and then nothing. Now I see one every once in a while and I still think it's Mitch. One night about 2 weeks after he died I was standing outside looking up at the stars. I said "Mitchell, if you're up there…. I miss you…." And after standing there a moment or two, I heard in my head CLEAR as day and in his voice, "I'm so fucking happy up here, Liz."

This is how my brother would have talked and he is one of the ONLY people who calls me Liz. I know it was him. I know what I heard and I know it was him.

***

Terri Harlow grew up in a beautiful Victorian home in the town of Baldwinsville, Massachusetts. Her parent's purchased it in the 1960's and spent the rest of their lives remodeling it. They loved the house like a family member.

Built in the 1880's, the house had its own carriage house, along with a massive old barn. The rooms were standard Victorian faire, with sitting rooms and parlors instead of living rooms and family rooms. Given its age, it came as no surprise to anyone that the house also came with a few ghosts.

Even though the rest of the family often felt the presence of lingering spirits, her mother frequently saw them. On their first night there, she watched as a woman rushed past her bed and disappeared into a window. The woman was so real and so close, her dress brushed against Terri's mother's arm as she lay in bed.

Another time, Terri's mother saw her own mother standing in the kitchen doorway. She was dressed up in a pretty dress and was wearing lipstick. She raised her arm over her head and asked, "Are you coming?" before she disappeared completely.

Terri is no stranger to the paranormal world herself. Having been an intuitive and paranormal investigator for many years, she's seen and experienced her fair share of strange occurrences. None struck her as profoundly as the appearance of her father one night.

Her father was a military policeman who served in Korea. He was a handsome man with jet black hair. After his military service ended, he worked at the local paper mill, operating their computer.

Terri remembers seeing the computer as a child. "It took up an entire wall, it was so large," she said. The computer ran everything in the mill and was one of the first computers of its kind.

After he died in 2001, the family felt the loss heavily. He was a good man and a kind father. When he visited her years later, she wasn't overly surprised he would make the effort.

While her mother was in the hospital for a surgery, Terri came to stay at her house and slept on a sofa in the back sitting room. The first night she was there, she woke to something she will never forget.

A dark misty shape leaned over her. Before she could react, it gently touched her hand. The touch was abnormally cold, but felt loving at the same time.

Instinctively, she recoiled backwards, which in turn, scared the misty shape. It retreated to a corner and disappeared, leaving her wondering and remorseful. In her heart, she knew it was her father.

As she stared at the corner, where the mist had disappeared, she felt the emotions sweep over her. The touch had been gentle, the kind of touch a father would give his sleeping daughter. Even though the misty shape had been terrifying to wake up to, she felt the sensation of love. It was as though he was saying, "This is my daughter." She wanted it to come back, but it didn't. It was one of the most memorable experiences she's ever had.

Terri's mother was also in the military, serving as a cryptographer. She was a member of the Women's Army Corp (WAC), which was quite an honor, considering only certain women were chosen to be members. Being in the military was the happiest part of her life. She got to travel and meet new people, including Terri's father.

After her mother's death, nearly ten years ago, Terri often feels her mother nearby, as well. She doesn't necessarily receive physical signs, but feels her presence. She knows that her mother still supports her and is proud of her accomplishments. The signs she's received from them let her know that they are still very much a part of her life, whether she can see them or not.

***

I met Sharon Galloway when I wrote the book *Ruin of Souls*. She shared a story of her personal haunting with me that I included in the book. When I asked her if she had any experiences with deceased loved ones, she shared the following story with me.

Sharon's Story

It was hard for my mother. She lived to be ninety before the health industry decided it was time for her to die. (I am having this investigated by several government agencies, but that's another story.) It was hard for her for many reasons, but one of the main reasons it was so hard was that all of her friends had already passed on.

My mother was made of iron. I never would have survived what the health industry did to her. Even her own doctors bent over to big pharma and prescribed unusual amounts of medications that would have killed anyone else. They almost killed her in 2009 when they overdosed her on heart meds. She was in a coma for three days and came out of it OK, even though she was, at that time, eighty-three years old.

When the medical and health industry decided to kill my mother, as they had with my father who had died the year before, they put her in hospice and then surreptitiously, and illegally, put her in a medically induced coma. This was shocking to my brother and me as we were told she would only be there for about two weeks, and then get moved back to her assisted living. We did not expect anything like this.

My brother left Mom at the hospice, where she was eating, talking, and was ambulatory, and the next morning she was non-responsive and barely breathing.
As my mother lay there in "hospice," my brother and I would sit with her, and I would pray with her. My mother especially liked the Blessed Mother, so I concentrated on those prayers.

As I sat with my mother, I would feel and sort of see her mother, my Nana, and her sister, Aunt Jean, and her other sister, Aunt Gina. My mother was the only one left in her immediate family.

I felt the presence of my Nana most often, but I also felt Aunt Jean. Aunt Jean was my favorite Aunt , but she died when I was only eleven.

My mother died very early January 30, 2015, at about 5:30am.

My mother existed for nine days even though she was starved, dehydrated, and over medicated. So, not at deaths door, I would say.

At the moment of my mother's death, I was sort of asleep, lying in bed thinking about getting up and driving down to see her, when I heard a distinct tick, tick, tick...DING! It sounded like an old-style egg timer.

I saw and heard my mother shoot up to the sky to meet her mother and her sisters, and they all flew around in a happy circle. My mother and the women in her family were reunited, and they were very, very happy.

My Nana, probably like when they were growing up, stood there and watched her girls fly and play. They were all girls again.

I told you all about the horrors of hospice because apparently it is epidemic. And, it's also part of my mother's story.

I am relieved that my mother, once again, prevailed and overcame the burden of the medical communities' abuse to be happy, and free.

***

Twana McRae's story doesn't involve a grandfather standing at the foot of her bed, but was provoking nonetheless.

Several days after her grandmother died in 1998, her aunt and uncle were working on a project in their basement.

As they worked, they were startled by a loud boom. It was a strange sound. In some ways, it sounded almost like a door slamming shut with the exception of the intensity of the sound. It was far louder than the normal sound a door makes when it bangs shut.

They looked at each other. Surely if someone had driven up, they would have heard the tires on the gravel driveway. There really was no way someone could make it to the door like that without being heard.

Then, out of the blue, they heard the distinct sound of her grandmother's voice.

"Anybody home?" she asked, just like her grandmother would have done, something Twana heard her do a hundred times as a child.

They ran upstairs, but no one was there. They shared the story for years, never finding any way to explain it. In their hearts they knew that Grandma came back for one last visit.

***

Jan Smith is another personal friend with an amazing story. When she shared it with me, it brought tears to my eyes as I considered the fact that love has no boundaries.

Jan's Story

I always had a problem waking up to an alarm clock and would usually sleep right through it. My husband would make sure I was awake at 5:30am before he left. When he died, I was afraid that I would have the same problem.

The first few mornings when I went back to school were very restless nights, and I was able to get up by 5:30. I should have mentioned that if I didn't get up at 5:30 and he didn't hear me stirring, he wouldn't come upstairs but would YELL my name and say it's 6 o'clock.

After about one week after I had gone back to school and managed to get up on time, I overslept. I awoke to his voice YELLING my name. I looked at the clock, it was exactly 6am. This happened a couple more times with it being exactly 6am.

He used to get up about 4:30 or 5:00 and go downstairs but would lovingly come back up to wake me at 5:30.

***

Danielle was only four years-old when her paternal grandmother died. She barely knew her and could count the times she saw her on one hand due to the fact that her father was in the military and they often lived in another state.

Nearly two years after her grandmother's death, her father retired so they could move back home to take care of her grandfather, whose health was beginning to decline.

From the age of six until she was thirteen, Danielle refused to use the bathroom alone in his house. Every time she went in there, she would see a lady standing in the shower. She always wore a blue robe and had blue fuzzy house slippers on her feet. The woman just stood there and stared at her. Nothing in her expression was menacing, but it frightened Danielle nonetheless.

Years later, Danielle happened upon a photo of a woman and was astounded at the resemblance to the woman in the shower.

"Who is this?" she asked her parents and was told that it was her grandmother. She truly wishes she would have known that when she was younger. Instead of retreating in fear, she might have tried to talk with her.

After her grandfather died, they sold the house. She still passes it frequently and wishes she could knock on the door and go inside so she can talk to her grandmother.

***

Amy Christensen came to one of my Paranormal 101 classes to share her story with me. As she told me about her experiences with her late mother, the entire class was mesmerized.

Amy's mom had cancer when she was a teenager. She passed away in 1979 when Amy was just fifteen years-old. The morning her mother passed away, the entire family was together in her room, except for Amy. She just wasn't ready to handle it, so she quietly excused herself and went to her own bedroom.

She sat down on her bed, her heart heavy with emotion. Losing a mother at any age was brutal, but losing her mother at fifteen was beyond heart-breaking. Her mind flooded with anguish. Her mother wouldn't see her graduate from high school nor would she be there when Amy got married and had children. It wasn't fair.

Her older sister came and sat on the bed with her. As they sat there silently sobbing, they felt a soft brush of air pass between them. Amy looked up, startled to see her mother floating outside her bedroom window.

"Don't be sad. I'm happy now," her mother told them. "Tell everybody I love them."

As the apparition of their mother slowly faded away, they looked at each other in stunned disbelief.

"Did you see that?" her sister asked her.

"I did," she said as tears streamed down both their faces.

After that, from January 1979 through Amy's freshmen year in college in the fall of 1981, she would frequently have conversations with her mother. If she needed something, she could hear her mother answer her. To her, it sounded like it was said aloud, but it never happened around anyone else. If she needed her mom, she was there to offer advice and encouragement.

One night some time later, she was lying in bed and felt something touch her foot. She woke up and saw her mother standing beside her bed. She told Amy she was leaving because Amy didn't need her any more. Amy cried and begged her to stay, but she hasn't had contact with her since.

Amy later found out that on her mother's deathbed, her mother told her father that out of all their children, she was most concerned about Amy.

Amy is highly intuitive, something I experienced firsthand after meeting her, but she closes down that part of herself. Much of it is due to a change in religious practices. When she became "born again," she felt that attempting to communicate with deceased loved ones went against what her church taught, so she ignored any signs she might have gotten.

She now understands there is more than "the rules" of religion. It's really all connected. Her faith is still very much fear based, but she's far more open to communication now than she was before, especially after her twin sister died in 2007.

While she hasn't felt anything close to what she felt when her mother visited, she sometimes feels as though her sister is nearby and it gives her a measure of comfort.

Amy shared another story with me regarding her work as a nurse at a nursing home.

Catherine was a long term resident who enjoyed joking around with the nurses. She always talked about "breaking out" in jest, but her condition was terminal and she wasn't long for this world.

A few minutes after she passed away, Amy was at the nurse's station when the front door flew open and the alarms went off. The entry to the nursing home was comprised of a double door system, with the alarm on the inner door. The only way for the alarm to go off was if someone opened the inner door. Both doors blew open at the same time.

All of the nurses bolted towards the doors, thinking that a patient had left the building, but when they got to the entrance, they were stunned. No one was there. They stood there for a moment, perplexed. This was something that had never happened before and it happened right after Catherine passed away.

Amy smiled to herself, wondering if Catherine finally got her wish and broke out.

***

Crystal Pina also worked in a nursing home. During her time there, she met a variety of personalities. Most of the residents were pleasant and gracious for the care they received, but one old man stood out from the crowd.

Leo was known as the "difficult patient." If someone brought him food, it wasn't warm enough. If someone came to give him his medication, he fought with them. Crystal was the only one he seemed to like.

When she cared for him, he often smiled at her and thanked her for what she did. The two began talking and she learned a lot about his life, helping her to understand some of his anger.

One day she took Leo aside and asked him why he was nice to her but was mean to everyone else. He told her it was because she treated him with respect. When she came into his room, she talked to him, asked his opinion on things and made him feel like a person and not just a patient. It made her feel good to hear that. She tried to always treat the patients with the dignity and respect they deserved.

A few months after Leo passed away, the nursing home hit on hard times. The funding they received was no longer enough to sustain the facility. It was going to close down.

All the people who worked there were worried because they knew they would lose their jobs. Crystal wasn't sure how she was going to make ends meet without it.

One night Crystal had a dream. In it, Leo came to her and told her not to worry that everything was going to be okay.

As it turns out, Leo's message was correct. The nursing home closing was actually a blessing for her. Her son became ill and required surgery. Because of his condition, she began receiving government assistance, which allowed her to stay home and take care of him.

***

(Above: Maria De Fatima's grandmother)

Maria De Fatima, who shared a story about a cardinal with me in an earlier chapter, also shared a story about her grandmother.

Her grandmother passed away when she was thirteen years-old. The night she passed away, Maria heard a knock on the door. She told her mother and they opened the door, only to find the doorstep empty. No one was there.

A few minutes later, it happened again. Maria called out to her mother, who told her to answer the door. When Maria opened the door, her grandmother was floating on the doorstep, nearly a foot off the ground.

She smiled and waved at Maria and then disappeared. Moments later, the phone rang. It was the hospital informing them of her grandmother's death. It's something Maria will never forget.

***

Rebecca Robshaw also had a personal greeting from her grandmother, but hers had a more humorous aspect to it.

One night she was in the kitchen washing dishes at the sink when she felt a sharp pinch on her backside. She whirled around, fully expecting to see someone in the room with her, but the room was empty.

It reminded her of her grandmother, who was in the hospital. When she and her brother were younger, her grandmother would sometimes pinch them on the bottom as a joke.

She told her husband that she thought her grandmother had died. The next morning, she received a call, confirming her suspicions. She still feels her grandmother's presence on occasion and believes that she is looking out for her.

Jeff Torgalski shared a touching story about the communication he had with his father who died in August of 2012.

His father had cancer of the throat, jaw and prostate and had been in and out of remission for nearly thirteen years. After a while, he began getting blood clots, which required amputation of several of his body parts.

When they first found the cancer back in the 1990's, it was supposed to be an easy procedure, but it didn't end up that way. He ended up losing his voice box during surgery, which reduced his capacity for speech.

A stubborn man, he refused to relearn speech, except for a few phrases. Depending on his condition and how he felt, sometimes the words consisted entirely of profanity. The day after his surgery, the only thing he said clearly was his favorite F word.

Above) Jeff's father with Jeff when he was younger

By 2012, he had basically given up. He needed more amputations and scopes to drain the food he ate because it just sat in his stomach. At that point, he confessed to Jeff that he wanted to die. His health began declining almost immediately.

On the night he died, his feeding tube backed up and he started leaking fluids from every orifice. His mother told Jeff to call 911, something his father profusely fought against. As they loaded him into an ambulance, he told Jeff that he was an asshole.

The next day, they planned on running tests. His mother was going to bring Jeff to the hospital later to see his father. As he was getting ready to leave, the phone rang. The Caller ID identified the call as coming from the hospital.

At first, Jeff thought it was his mother, calling to give him an update on his father, but the line was filled with static. The only word he could clearly make out was the word "asshole," the same name his father called him as he was being loaded into the ambulance. He hung up the phone, not knowing how to interpret what he just heard.

An hour later, he got another call from the hospital. This time, it was his mother on the line, telling him that his father had passed away. After bringing him back from his CT-scan, he stopped breathing and couldn't be revived. Jeff realized that the first call he received from the hospital came at the precise moment his father stopped breathing.

The loss of his father hit him hard. Even though his father was often gruff with him, he felt the loss deeply. It seemed so strange knowing he wouldn't be around any longer.

That night, Jeff went into the kitchen to get a drink of water. As he passed his father's recliner, he noticed a strange mist floating on the chair. When his father was home, it was always his favorite spot in the house. As Jeff stared at the mist in the chair, trying to make sense of what he was seeing, the chair suddenly began rocking back and forth. Jeff then heard his father's voice.

"Asshole," the voice said and then added his father's favorite F word.

At first, Jeff thought his father was haunting him because continued to see the mist and hear the words nightly. He was surprised months later when he happened upon several remembrances his father left behind.

One was a deck of pinochle cards, which was his favorite game. His father had always been deadly serious about playing pinochle. He often shouted and swore during the game. Jeff was the only person he would take as a partner. It was definitely a sign that he was still there.

Perhaps, what was more thought provoking was what he found inside the deck of cards. It was a letter from his father. In it, his father talked about how much he loved his four boys and how out of all his boys, he was the most proud of Jeff. As Jeff read it, tears came to his eyes. His father never shared his feelings with him. He also found several photos of them together, that felt like gift wrapping on a thoughtful present.

The year before his father's passing, Jeff and his mother purchased a small Christmas tree to place beside his father's recliner for him to enjoy. While his father was alive, the tree struggled to stay alive and hardly grew at all. After his death, the tree took on new life. Despite all obstacles, it tree grew and flourished to the point where it needed to be repotted. Jeff told me that he will need to replant it outdoors if it grows any larger.

As someone who is sensitive to paranormal activity, Jeff often has to contend with hauntings in his house. It isn't out of his normal realm to see dark shadows flitting across the walls and feel the presence of someone from beyond the grave.

One night, Jeff saw a dark shadow moving across his bedroom wall. He didn't like the way it made him feel. As he attempted to get away from it, his room filled with a bright light. The light was so intense, it blinded him for a moment. As his eyes adjusted, he saw the image of his father standing inside of it with a broad smile on his face. Almost immediately, the dark shadow vanished and his room returned to normal.

"I still see him, but at least I know he's not haunting me," Jeff said.

Jeff also has had several encounters with his grandmother, who died in September of 2015 "Gram and I always had tradition that during holidays and birthdays we'd always get each other lottery tickets and split the winnings. Plus, no matter how sick she was, or if she was out of town, she'd always call me to wish me a happy birthday," he said.

Two weeks before she passed away, he began getting horrible headaches. He later learned that his grandmother died from over a hundred mini-strokes, with the pain being similar to what he felt. Was this his grandmother's way of letting him know what she was enduring?

He went to see her the day she died and brought her their traditional lottery tickets. Once he took a look at her, he could tell that it wouldn't be long. She didn't look good. That night, as he was trying to fall asleep, the lights dimmed in his room and he saw a mist hover near his bed. An hour later, he received a phone call, telling him that she had passed away. Even though he didn't get a clear vision of his grandmother, he knew it was her, coming to say goodbye.

As it turns out, his grandmother *(pictured to the left with Jeff and his grandfather)* still had one last message to give him. His birthday fell shortly after her death. When the phone rang, the Caller ID was blank. He answered it anyway and was surprised to hear a recording of someone singing happy birthday to

165

him. Was it his grandmother, continuing her tradition from the grave?

He'll never know for sure, but he still purchases lottery tickets on special holidays in her honor. This past Christmas, he told her, "Grams, we're going to split it like usual." That night he saw the distinct image of his grandmother and his father standing in the living room near his father's recliner, smiling at him.

Later that night, when he scratched the lottery tickets, he discovered that he won twenty-four dollars, the exact same amount they won together the last time they played. He still continues to see both of them on occasion, something that brings a measure of comfort to his life.

Most people who wish to communicate with deceased loved ones would love the opportunities that Jeff has experienced. Unfortunately, this doesn't happen for most people. Part of the reason might be due to Jeff's affinity to see and communicate with ghosts and spirits. It's something he has experienced all his life, a gift he shared with his grandmother.

As a paranormal investigator and the founder of Southern Indiana Paranormal Investigations (SIPI) Billy Miller is no stranger to paranormal encounters, but one of them hit close to home.

When Billy Miller's mother got sick from congestive heart failure in 2000, they installed a hospital bed in their home for her to use. Nurses would come in and take care of her and give her medicine several times a day, making her as comfortable as possible.

She tried to sit up in her chair lift, but the drain of her illness often required her to retreat to her hospital bed. When her husband came home from work, she would often plead for him to lie down beside her. After so many years of marriage, she was more comfortable having him in the bed with her.

Unfortunately, due to the size of the bed, they wouldn't comfortably fit in it together. She would often plead for him to at least try and he would squeeze himself in and stay until she fell asleep.

A month after she passed away, his father came home from work one evening and climbed into his bed, exhausted. He always lay on his side to sleep, but when he tried to roll over, he could feel a body pressed snugly behind him. As he stiffened with horror, he heard the distinct sound of his late wife's moan. She remained there for about thirty minutes before she disappeared. Just like old times, she wanted him to lay with her .

***

After her father died, Barbara Kirk Niles wanted her mother to move in with her. She was afraid that her mother would be too lonely living by herself. She also wanted to have her close so she could take care of her.

(Above) Barbara Kirk Niles with her father

Growing up, Barbara had eight brothers and sisters. Her mother spent her entire childhood selflessly taking care of everybody. It was the least that Barbara could do to repay her.

The first month her mother was at her house, Barbara slept in the bed with her to make sure she was okay. As soon as the lights were turned off, they began hearing strange tapping sounds. When Barbara got up to look, she realized the sounds were coming from the ribbon from her father's funeral wreath. It said "Husband."

After the first month passed, Barbara returned to her own bed, satisfied that her mother would be okay sleeping alone. Not long after, Barbara's mother began feeling the sensation of someone climbing into bed with her. After 52 years of marriage, it was a feeling that was familiar to her. It felt exactly like her husband was climbing into bed with her. She wasn't frightened by the encounter. She knew who it was.

As it turns out, it wouldn't be the last sign of her father.

Two years after her father died, Barbara found herself in blinding pain. Her stomach had been bothering her for four years, but she had been able to push the pain aside. This time though, it was too much to bear. She felt as though her father was nudging her.

"You have to go. You have to go!" a voice told her inside her head. She knew it was her father, so she went to the hospital and ended up having emergency surgery for her gallbladder. If she hadn't gone then, she would have died.

When she came home from the hospital, she slept downstairs in her mother's bed, since her mother was away, visiting family in Nevada. As she closed her eyes and started to drift off to sleep, she felt the sensation of someone climbing into bed with her. She smiled.

"Thanks, Dad," she whispered, acknowledging his message.

Two years later, her father came to the rescue again, although Barbara is fairly certain he was behind the mischief to begin with.

While he was alive, Barbara's father was something of a practical joker. He especially liked to tease Barbara's nephew Justin.

When Justin came to stay with Barbara for several weeks while he was in the process of moving, he had a curious experience.

He knew he put his wallet on the dresser, but the next morning, it was missing. He looked all around the house for it, even enlisting Barbara into the search.

After they searched the house, the wallet was nowhere to be found. Barbara forgot about it until three weeks later when Justin brought it up again.

"Aunty, I still can't find my wallet," he said.

Barbara thought about it for a moment and it all clicked into place as she remembered her father's fondness for playing pranks.

"Ask Pappa where it is," she told him.

Justin followed her advice and was amazed the next morning. His wallet was back on his dresser.

A gift doesn't have to be something purchased from a store. It could be a cherished moment or an act of serendipity. Have you ever been feeling down and then received a friendly call from a friend to see how you're doing? Or perhaps your melancholy thoughts might have been interrupted by the sight of a beautiful cardinal landing on your fence post outside your window or a perfectly centered feather on your front door mat. Another gift could be a flower blooming out of season or a perfect white feather on your door stop.

For me, one of the greatest gifts I've ever received came to me on Mother's Day in 2012. I was feeling especially down. My grown kids made a brief visit to see me, but had work obligations for the rest of the day, leaving me home by myself. Since my own mother was a thousand miles away in Indiana, I moped around the house all day. I walked outside to get some fresh air and discovered a baby squirrel sitting on my step. Orphaned and abandoned, he needed the one thing I needed to give: mothering. I bottle fed him and eventually released him back into the wild, never doubting this was a gift from a loved one.

My mother also received an unexpected gift from beyond the grave.

For years, my mother and her friend Sue were like peas in a pod. They were always together, often out shopping or going out to eat. I met Sue a few times and could understand my mother's draw to her.

Sue had a warm smile that was nearly a permanent expression on her face. She was friendly and outgoing to everyone she met. When she began having stomach pains and learned she had late stage stomach cancer, my mother was devastated

She accompanied Sue to all of her doctor's appointments and kept her spirits high with shopping outings. One of their excursions found them at the grocery store.

It was close to Thanksgiving and the store had a display of white ceramic gravy bowls that were shaped like cows. Both my mother and Sue had gravy boats at home and certainly didn't need another one, but they were so taken by the cow-shaped boats, they both purchased one. As it would turn out, that was Sue's last Thanksgiving.

After her death, my mother was at a loss. Signs of Sue were everywhere, from songs on the radio to the places they used to enjoy going. Sue's absence left a tremendous hole in her life and she felt the loss with the heaviest of hearts.

She didn't think about the cow-shaped gravy boats they purchased together until the following Thanksgiving. My mother opened the cabinet where she kept it and discovered two boats instead of one. There was no doubt in her mind that Sue had presented her with a gift that was undeniable.

She still misses Sue and thinks about her often, but knowing that Sue is still around watching over her gives her a measure of comfort. It's a friendship that survived death.

***

Billy Miller was nine or ten when his grandpa passed away in the mid 1960's. His grandfather was a robust man with immense determination. Despite the fact that he was paralyzed from the waist down, he still managed to build the house they lived in. He even hung the shingles on the roof.

After he passed away, the families found themselves in a serious hardship. Money was scarce, especially without his income. If something didn't happen soon they would lose the house he built.

Billy's grandma went to bed one night, thoughts of losing the house filling her mind. As she started to drift off to sleep, something made her open her eyes. She stared across the room, astounded to see her late husband materializing in front of his closet.

He was wearing his favorite jacket. It was an old motorcycle jacket with various zippered pockets, something that was in style back then. He didn't own a motorcycle, but he loved the jacket. He wore it all the time. As she stared at him, he slowly faded back into the closet. He appeared five nights in a row and would stand in front of the closet long enough for her to see him before he faded away again.

One night he appeared and she said, "Pete what are you doing here? What do you want to tell me?"

He just stood in front of the closet, watching her.

Something triggered in her mind at that moment. She climbed out of bed and went to the closet. Inside of it, she found his old motorcycle jacket, the same one he kept appearing in. As her fingers fumbled nervously, she unzipped one of the pockets. Inside was a wad of cash. She quickly opened the other pockets and found more money stashed in them as well.

She ended up finding thousands of dollars, which was enough to save the house. She squealed in delight as she realized what her beloved Pete had done for them. He saved the house.

He never came back again after that and the family went on to live in the house for years to come.

Raymond Richard shared the following story with me.

Ray's Story

My friend Paul passed in mid-2001. He knew about and experienced my spiritual gifts. At that time I only did readings with Tarot Cards and was recently attuned as a Reiki Master teacher. He was a good friend and was curious about all this spiritual stuff. He thought it was creepy at times. Paul wasn't interested in learning any of it. This was a time before all the TV shows we now have about this stuff. Our mutual lady friend Gerry, who was a counselor at the local Veteran Outreach Center, used this stuff, but specialized in hypnosis and past life regression. We three were very connected spiritually through many lifetimes.

Paul had a severe addiction to recreational drugs then. He would be clean for long periods. But he said "it was like a sleeping lion within him that would wake, roar and Paul would be addicted again. One night he was high at a party and someone gave him something that added to what he was on all ready. He overdosed and passed away easily, peacefully that night.

A few days after his funeral, Paul's Spirit gifted me white feathers every day for a couple weeks after his passing. With each pure white feather, I could feel his loving essence joy. I felt comforted. This helped me feel peace joy, thankful for knowing him.

Only white feathers would fall 0ne to two feet directly in front of me. Each white delicate beauty would drift slowly from above, flowing down in front of me, drifting down in a straight vertical direction to the ground. It did not matter whether there was a breeze or wind. Each white feather would fall as if it was in its own world and the outside world could not touch it during this journey down to the earth.

I felt as if, he, the feather was smiling at me from down there on the ground.

***

Dana Boadway Masson attends my Paranormal 101 online classes and shared the following story with me.

Dana's Story

I was visiting my parents last year, with my toddler in tow. One morning, as I was in the bathroom getting dressed and ready for company to come over, I had taken off my wedding rings and put them on the bathroom counter so that I could put on makeup etc. without getting them dirty.

My son came in, poked around a bit, got under my feet a bit, and then left when I asked him to go see grandma so I could finish what I was doing. When I went to put my rings back on, my wedding band was missing.

This ring is SO important to me. Not only is it MY wedding band, but it was also my paternal grandmother's wedding band. And if you know my son, you know that he sticks small objects in just about any crack or crevice it will fit into, and immediately will forget where he put it. So I instantly panicked.

I asked him over and over and over if he knew where it was. "Did you take my ring off the counter?"

175

He said, "yes."

"Do you remember where you put it?" I asked him.

He replied with, "no."

I was searching the entire house, looking everywhere I could think of at his eye level and below.

My mom was very upset for me. She knew how heartbroken I would be if it wasn't found. While I was downstairs looking around, all of a sudden, I heard her cry out and then she was in tears. I came running upstairs to find out what had happened.

Once she pulled herself together a little bit, she told me: "I pulled out the table to look behind it. I had looked around, and swept out some dust bunnies, but didn't see it. I stood back, closed my eyes, and asked my mom (my other grandma) for help to find the ring.

My mom has told me often that she gets messages from her mom, who passed away only a year before.

Well, the second my mom requested help, she heard a "PING" down on the floor at her feet. She looked down, and there was my wedding band. That's when she burst into tears. What a wonderful confirmation of communication!

Later, my son explained to me that "Great Grandma found your ring, and now your heart isn't broken anymore!"

*W*hen people are close to passing, their loved ones who have passed before them often come and wait for them to pass, so they can personally escort them into the light. I've heard these stories over and over again, but none was more touching than the story my father shared about his own mother.

Grandma Stierley had a hip operation. It was supposed to be a routine operation, one that is performed hundreds of times a week at the hospital she was admitted to. Unfortunately, that wasn't to be the case. While she was in surgery, she had a massive stroke which put her in a coma.

The family sat vigil around her bed, hoping for the best, but there wasn't anything they could do for her. She just lay there on life support. After some time, the doctor recommended that they cut off the life support and allow her to pass. She wasn't ever going to get better. It would be best to let her go.

The family signed the paperwork and watched with heavy hearts as the life support was turned off. They sat and watched the monitors record her paces towards death.

The heart rate monitor began declining. It registered a heartbeat, which was followed by a long pause before the next beat came along. The time was near.

As tears flowed down their cheeks, they watched her, knowing they were all witnessing the last moments of her life. Just as they expected her to take her last breath, she did something astounding. She opened her eyes for the first time in weeks.

She didn't acknowledge anyone in the room. Instead, she seemed to be fixated on something in the far distance, something no one else in the room could see. Then, a beautiful smile warmed her face as though she saw something that made her very happy. She took her last breath, then closed her eyes and left us.

In my heart of hearts, I like to believe that she was seeing her husband Arthur, who had died several years previously, but it could have been any number of family members. All that counts is that they came to bring her home.

People have told me that both my Grandma and Grandpa Stierley watch over me. Psychic mediums have felt them near me, conveying messages about how proud they are of me for always trying to be a good person and for not giving up on my dreams.

On that day, the world lost a great woman but I gained a new guardian instead.

***

When Barbara Williams' father-in-law passed away, she too had an experience.

They normally spent Thanksgiving with her husband's parents, but one particular year, he wasn't feeling well, so he stayed at home. Barbara and her husband Steve met the rest of the family and then brought him back a plate filled with food afterwards.

When she came into his house, she knew right away that something was different. He had been sick for several years and his mental state was consistently based in confusion. This time though, he had an enormous sense of clarity about him. He was talking with everyone like he hadn't in years. Instead of just answering with yes and no answers, he was asking pertinent questions in response. As a registered nurse, Barbara knew this probably wasn't actually a good sign.

On the way home, she talked to Steve about it, explaining that this sometimes happens when people are near passing. She attributes this to what she calls a "step-in" which helps them make peace with their current lives to allow them to tie up loose ends so they can pass more easily.

Two weeks later, they got a call that her father-in-law was in the ICU in a coma. When they got there, the entire family was sitting around him in vigil.

Barbara knew that he could still hear them, so she suggested that they come into the room, one at a time, and say their goodbyes. After they were finished, they all returned to the room and sat as a group.

By about 3pm, Barbara's mother-in-law told everyone that she would need to leave by 5pm. Her eyesight wasn't good and she worried about driving in the dark.

They sat around for a few more hours. At about two minutes before five, her mother-in-law rose from her chair, getting ready to leave when something changed with him. Barbara could feel his vibration come to a standstill. At five o'clock on the dot, he passed away.

"This just goes to show that we are very individual and have some control about the time of our passing. We will go when we feel like going," Barbara said.

She also added that some people will wait for their family members to get there before they go, while others don't want an audience. "They'll wait until you get out of that room and go to the bathroom before they'll die," she said.

A few weeks later, Barbara's mother-in-law called to tell her she had the oddest dream. She could feel someone getting into bed with her. Not only had he respected her time request, he came back to say goodbye to her one last time.

***

Years ago, Cheryl Phillips attended the funeral of a friend who had passed away. While the priest was talking, there was a sudden interference on his microphone. It was so loud and startling, everyone in the church jumped at the sound. He tried to correct it, but long moments went by with the interference blaring. He commented to the congregation that he'd never experienced that before. Cheryl knew it was a sign from her friend.

According to many well-known psychic mediums, everybody attends their own funeral after they die. They will often roam around the room, offering comfort to their loved ones, trying to give them signs that they are peaceful in their passing.

***

While attending her grandfather's funeral, Marion Luoma also had an experience. As she was walking down the aisle after the service with her grandmother, a huge ray of sunshine beamed through the stained glass window and shined down on all of them. When they got outside, they were perplexed because the sky was filled with dark angry clouds and it was raining. She took it as a sign that her grandfather was there and was telling them that he was okay.

While most people are tuned inwards during funerals, absorbed in their own emotions, if they look outside of themselves, they might see the signs their loved ones are trying to give them. It could be a touch on the shoulder or a caress on the face or simply a fond memory playing in their minds.

Sandra Chase had an experience several days after her husband's funeral. She woke up one morning and smelled smoke ash. It was different from wood smoke and had a distinctive smell that made an immediate association in her mind. Her husband had been cremated, something he had requested prior to his death. Their plans were for her to be buried one day with his ashes so they could be together forever. She thought it was a confirmation that he was happy that his wishes had been granted.

***

For others, the sign of someone's passing follows a more emotional route.

Larry Sanchez was having an ordinary day. The weather was nice and he had the day planned out. If he got everything done, he was thinking of taking his motorcycle out for a spin. Without any warning, he felt an overwhelming sensation of rage come over him. He didn't know why it happened. It came out of the blue for no reason.

Seconds later, the phone rang. It was his sister calling to tell him that his grandmother had just passed away. As soon as he got the news, the sensation of anger washed away in an instant. Somehow he knew it was her letting him know she'd gone.

***

In some situations the signs don't come at the funeral, but happen later in the day. For Tami Sansoucie, she received confirmation after they got back home from her grandfather's funeral.

As a paranormal investigator, Tami was watching closely for signs of his presence during the funeral and was a bit dismayed not to see anything. The family went to the house afterwards. They spent some time, just talking about her grandfather and the wonderful memories they had of him.

Out of the blue, they heard three loud bangs inside the house. They weren't sounds she had ever heard in the house before. It was summer, so it wouldn't have come from the hot water pipes.

The family went inside to look for the source of the sounds, but couldn't find anything that would explain it. Tami instinctively knew it was him saying goodbye to them.

Chapter 17 – When Nothing Happens

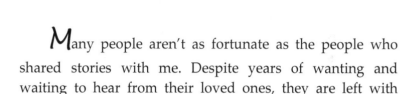

Many people aren't as fortunate as the people who shared stories with me. Despite years of wanting and waiting to hear from their loved ones, they are left with silence.

According to Barbara Williams, people we've had a close bond with are always around us.

"Our space is very crowded," she said. "But, they don't interfere. They have things to do on the other side too. It's not like they're standing there twiddling their thumbs."

When asking for signs, always keep an open mind while you look for it. The signs might not be exactly as you expect. For example, if you ask to see a white bird as a sign that your mother is around and you don't live near the coast, the white bird might come in another form. You might see a white bird on a greeting card or on a billboard as you're driving to work instead. Don't let your expectations cloud your experience.

After you've asked for a sign, watch the world around you with careful eyes. If you have an item that once belonged to your relative, place it in a location where you can readily see it. Dismiss all preconceived notions of what you thought a message would look like.

When something happens that is out of the ordinary, make note of it. Write it down and research it. If you see a hummingbird at your window and it brings a thought to mind, pursue it. Did your mother love hummingbirds? Also watch for signs that stand out, like a rose blooming in the middle of the winter or the smell of pipe tobacco in your living room.

Lower your expectations for what a sign should look like. Not everyone will see a full-bodied apparition in her bedroom, pointing towards the location of hidden money. Most people will see things like an annoying moth that won't go away or a thought that touches their minds at the right moment.

If you're still having issues connecting with a deceased loved one, talk to a psychic medium to help you make the connection. A good psychic medium can help you understand the signs you've been receiving.

The important thing is to never give up. Even if you don't receive a sign, that doesn't mean your loved one isn't around you. Talk to him and let him know how you feel, while you know in your heart that the message was received.

Rest assured, your loved ones are there. Always.

Psychic Medium Barbara Williams can be found at www.Barbarawilliamsphd.com

About the Author

Joni Mayhan is a paranormal investigator and author who teaches a Paranormal 101 class, both online and in the town of Gardner, Massachusetts. She was born and raised in southern Indiana, but has spent the last thirty years living in Massachusetts.

She has two grown children and a house filled with spoiled pets.

When she's not writing, teaching or communicating with dead people, Joni loves reading, exploring new places and meeting new friends. To learn more about Joni or to read her paranormal blog, check out her website: Jonimayhan.com.

Please continue reading for a sample of *Dark and Scary Things – A Sensitive's Guide to the Paranormal World*

Spirit Nudges

Allowing Help from the Other Side

By

Joni Mayhan

Introduction

We've all been there.

The world comes down so hard on us, we want to hide in a hole until the pressure eases. We are forced to make rapid-fire decisions, but are only vaguely aware of which direction we should turn. Should I take that job and move across the country? Did I make the right decision in getting married? Should I trust my friend with this secret? What should I do?

Imagine for a minute that you have many of the answers at your fingertips. All you have to do is learn how to access them. It's not a button that you press or a file that you read; it's something that is already built into your spiritual makeup, a part of you that you might not be tuned into.

I call them nudges.

I've been getting them all my life, but the first one I truly remember occurred when I was ten years old.

I was somewhat of a willful child, one prone to pushing the boundaries. If my mother told me to be inside the house by the time it got dark, I came in mere seconds after the street lights illuminated. When I found a stray collie dog wandering the neighborhood, I hid it in our garage until I was discovered. The word no was a starting place for me, not an ending.

One night as my mother was cooking dinner, she emphatically told me that I wasn't allowed to eat any snacks before dinner. She was making fried chicken and was tired of seeing me pick at my food because I'd filled up on cookies beforehand.

As the chicken sizzled in the skillet, my mother left the kitchen to answer a phone call. Once she was gone from the room, I eyed the cookie jar sitting on the counter.

One cookie wouldn't hurt anything, right?

I had my hand out, reaching for the cookie jar when I heard a voice inside my head.

"Don't do that!" it said. The voice sounded vaguely like my grandmother's voice with a tone that was almost conspiratorial. She wasn't yelling at me like my mother would have done. She simply didn't want me to get caught. I dropped my arm in an instant and jolted around to glance behind me.

My grandmother wasn't there, which would have been very odd, considering she'd been dead for four years, but I wasn't alone. My mother had pulled the phone cord to the kitchen doorway and was silently watching me with arched eyebrows.

"You weren't getting into those cookies, were you?" she asked.

I feigned innocence and reached past the cookie jar to the crock of spoons. I selected the first one my trembling fingers landed on and moved to the stove, where I began stirring the boiling potatoes, my mind racing.

Who had tipped me off?

Was it my grandmother? The thought sent a chill racing down my spine. If it was my grandmother, did that make her a ghost? I wasn't sure what to make of it. The only thing I knew was that she had helped me when I needed her assistance. As it turns out, it wouldn't be the first time.

My grandmother, along with an entire army of spiritual allies, has helped me all my life. They've steered me away from bad relationships, prevented me from getting into accidents and have helped me find the path I was intended to follow. All I had to do was listen to the nudges.

It all starts with one word: *believe*.

Believe

If you are someone who only believes what you see with your own eyes, this book will be a waste of your time. Put it away and move onto the rest of your life. Come back to it when you're ready, because you have to believe before it will work.

Belief comes with an open mind, one that is willing to consider options that aren't carved in stone. You have to stretch the boundaries between what you've been taught and what you feel in your soul and allow the spark of insight a place to furrow. This is much more than Tinkerbell's magic dust, it's a concept that our minds can't fully comprehend. The world is much broader than the physical compositions we can experience with our five traditional senses.

Once you allow yourself to believe, you open up a part of yourself that provides you with access to the help you need. I think of it like a transmitter. If the switch is turned off, you won't be able to communicate. Belief is the on button. Doubt is the button that turns it all off.

Psychic Medium Brandie Wells does gallery readings several times a week in her community of Keene, New Hampshire. "I'm connecting with people in a circle and I can feel their energy. A lot of times, I know when people are blocking me or are resisting me. That resistance makes it difficult for them to receive messages. When they're already closed off, they don't understand that their resistance actually creates a block," she said.

She also feels that people don't always see the signs. "If you came in completely innocent and were taught to pay attention to these signs, you would notice them, but we're not," she said.

When we open ourselves up to a spiritual way of life, we begin to see our lives in a much broader spectrum. We begin to see the synchronicities and how they create a pathway for us to follow. We understand that the things that happen to us in our lives are lessons and not punishments. We aren't supposed to get everything we ask for. We are supposed to struggle. The more we struggle, the more we learn.

We begin to understand that everything we encounter has a purpose. Everything happens for a reason. We might see the reason immediately, but many times we never see it at all. I think of it as the Domino Effect.

The Domino Effect

Imagine this scenario. You wake up one morning and go outside to start your car. When you turn the key, nothing happens. The battery is dead.

You can't believe this is happening to you. You have so much to do at work. You can't have a delay.

You call the mechanic shop down the street and ask them to come give you a jump start. By the time you make your way to work, two hours have passed and you're late getting started. It ruins your entire day.

What you don't realize is that the reason for the delay might have actually saved your life. Someone leaving a night shift might have run a red light. Had you been at that precise intersection at your normal time, you might have been broadsided, sending you to the hospital or possibly even ending your life. Or, the mechanic you called might have been struggling to pay his bills. Your call gave him the money he needed to make a payment on his electric bill before it was shut off. Or perhaps it was due to something more personal. Perhaps, someone came to work with a fever and then left before you got there, preventing you from getting sick. Or it could have been as simple as the smile you gave someone on the sidewalk that changed their entire day.

The best way to see the Domino Effect is to look at it in hindsight.

I've had many Domino Effects in my life, but the one that stands out the clearest is the cataclysmic destruction of a dream.

After working in the pet industry for several years, I dreamed of opening my own shop. It would be small, but filled to the brim with charm. I would have handcrafted bamboo bird cages filled with colorful finches, custom aquariums shaped like coffee tables and walls filled with useful pet items. I mapped out a floorplan, found distributors to purchase my product from and even found the perfect location. All I needed was the financing.

I spent long nights pouring over my business plan. There wasn't a detail I didn't examine. I imagined myself standing behind the counter, chatting with pet owners, answering their questions. I would no longer be required to work for someone else, carrying out instructions that didn't make any sense to me. I wouldn't be forced to work the shifts that no one else wanted to work. I would make the rules and I would prosper. Every time I thought about it, I smiled. It was all I wanted.

My dream came to an abrupt end when I took my plans to the bank and asked for a business loan. They applauded me for my carefully crafted plans, but wouldn't loan me the money unless I put my house down as equity for the loan. I walked away heartbroken.

I didn't see the reason for my failure for several months. The anchor store in the plaza where I wanted to put my pet shop went out of business. Soon afterwards, nearly every store in the plaza closed as a result. Mine would have been one of them. I would have lost my house, my money and all my carefully laid out plans.

Instead, I went back to work for another company and quickly rose through the ranks, finding a place to flourish and grow, while learning the business. It was where I needed to be until I was ready to move onto another endeavor.

Last summer I encountered another synchronicity that falls soundly into the Domino Effect category. I was invited to attend an online meeting for a paranormal group out of New Mexico. I was thrilled to be involved in the meeting and met some amazing people. One of these people was Skeeter Welhouse, who shared the following story with me.

Skeeter's Story

Skeeter experienced a Domino Effect several years ago after she moved from New Mexico to Washington State. Soon after moving there, she felt compelled to join a new paranormal team in her new state. Through the experience, she was introduced to individuals on the team who embraced her abilities as a psychic medium and encouraged her to continue her studies.

Her new group members invited her to a metaphysical market, where she would conduct psychic readings for people. While she had never done public readings before, she decided to give it a try. The experience was life altering for her. It gave her the opportunity to fully explore her abilities and meet others with similar skills.

During the same time period, she opened her own seamstress business. While she enjoyed the work, it wasn't apparently part of her life's path. Soon after the Christmas season, the business began failing. Once she made the decision to close the business, her psychic endeavors began to take off. She was soon invited onto a radio show to act as the guest psychic and began getting requests from clients for paid psychic readings.

"With everything from this chain of event, I realized this was where I was supposed to go," she said. She began working on a metaphysical book and continues to do psychic readings.

"I don't know what happened, but moving to Washington from New Mexico almost a year and a half ago just catapulted me onto a path I never expected. I finally feel at home," she said.

***

Laura King also shared a story about her experiences with the Domino Effect.

Laura's Story

All my life, since a very young age, I felt I was missing my other half. I kept asking my grandma if I had an older brother who had died. When she told me no, I'd argue because I just knew it. Every so often I'd look up at the moon over the years and still feel "he" was out there, but where?

I knew there was another part of me I was missing. I gave up wondering and wanting over time. I married and had an okay life. In 1994 I became depressed and had no desire to go out anymore after losing my daughter Danielle.

While I was online one day, I saw a familiar name I hadn't thought of since 1988. It was my friend John. John and I became fast friends again and suddenly I wanted to go out. He flirted with me and made me feel attractive again. We started hanging out a few times a week. I enjoyed his company since we shared many interests. He soon introduced me to an online role playing game. I loved it and became addicted to it and became quick friends online with the guy Adam who ran it.

Adam and I started chatting and surfing the same websites online and he found this site called Cybertown. It was a 3D chat world in which you sign up and can go to different areas (they called it virtual worlds) and even take a job as a block deputy, etc., and be in charge of the chat areas. It was more complex, but I can't remember tech terms. Anyway Adam and I hung out there awhile and it felt good socializing again even if it was just online. It helped me get confidence in myself again and I felt like I could venture out in the real world.

One day when I was hosting a chat in Cybertown, this guy Michael popped up and I fell madly in love with his personality. He made me feel attractive and cared for. Long story short, I left New York to be with him in Florida. I spent 16 years with Michael, through good and bad. Michael was a good guy, but he could be somewhat abusive. Michael was disabled and couldn't earn enough money, so I had to be strong and keep jobs that overwhelmed me.

I learned so much in my struggles in Florida. I learned how to stand on my own two feet, what *not* to do in a relationship and what I wanted in life. One day in 2010, Michael started using Facebook. He told me it was kind of cool, so I joined.

I soon became friends with this guy Kevin on Facebook. I thought Kevin was cute but had many issues going on in his life. I quickly unfriended him, because, at the time, I had too much on my plate with Michael's abuse. I'd become depressed and had given up on relationships by this time.

Then in November of 2015, I saw a post from a friend on Facebook. As I read the responses, I saw Kevin's name. I was amazed he survived his health issues.

I was tempted to friend him, but I wasn't sure it was wise with everything I'd been through. I had a feeling we would become involved. That scared me since I felt it was going to be very intense. I didn't want the drama from another relationship. I told myself if I ran into him again, I would friend request him as it would be fate.

A few weeks later in December, I saw another posted response of Kevin's. "That's it," I told myself. I sent Kevin a friend request. It was fate.

After that, every interaction with each other was very intense. I could see in my mind's eye we were going to be romantically involved. He told me he saw it too. Long story short, we must be soul mates or twin souls. We share so much in common and we are almost exactly alike.

Kevin told me as a child, he felt he had another half of him missing and he would look up at the moon wondering where his other half was. He told me this before I admitted what I used to do. So many things we felt and did that were alike it was mind blowing. Even the length of time in both of our relationships were the same. Every time Kevin had a breakup I had one at the same time. He's 4 years older than me but we were in sync though apart and didn't know each other.

A year later, in October of 2016, I moved in with Kevin and we became engaged. If I didn't find John, who led me to Adam, who led me to Michael, and then become friends with my Facebook friend Phil, Kevin and I would never have met.

I wish Kevin and I had met earlier, but I needed all the experiences to grow as did he.

Another Domino Effect in my life was in 1985 when I wished on a shooting star for a boyfriend. I was tired of being alone. The next day, one of the workers at my job came up and asked me out. His name was Jack and we dated for quite some time. I learned a lot from him.

After I learned that Jack cheated on me with another girl, the relationship was over. Not long afterwards, I ran into the girl he cheated on me with. Her name was Amanda. We somehow ended up becoming friends.

Amanda invited me to her home where I met her sister Sara. Sara and I became fast friends and she became like a sister to me. Though she was 4 years younger, she taught me so much and opened up my life in so many ways. Whenever we went out people looked at us and asked if we were sisters.

Sara and I parted for a few years, but one day she suddenly popped back in my life. We found out we did so many similar things during that time apart, even buying the same clothes! Sara helped me realize I was in a bad marriage. She was instrumental in that too. If I didn't meet Sara, I wouldn't have had the confidence to even approach my old friend John. I don't know if everyone has as many interconnecting experiences. I am thankful for mine.

***

Laura's story showcases the steps we often need to take to reach our goals. Sometimes the steps seem more like punishments than achievements, but when you zoom out and look at them as a whole, you can see the pattern emerge.

Domino Effects come in all shapes and sizes. Some of them are so profound, it's difficult to miss them, but others are subtle and easy to miss.

Spirit Nudges – Allowing Help from the Other Side can be found where you purchased this book.

69447685R00115

Made in the USA
San Bernardino, CA
15 February 2018